Start a Cake Business Today

By Paula Spencer

InformationTree Press

Middlebury VT, USA

Start a Cake Business Today

© 2008 by InformationTree
All rights reserved.

ISBN: 0-9816469-0-5

Printed in the United States of America.

Contents

START A CAKE BUSINESS TODAY

INTRODUCTION

Independent wedding cake businesses are often very successful. Small shops are able to provide more one-on-one specialized attention for their clients and are often willing to take on designs and ideas that commercial bakeries would not. Your decision to open a cake decorating business may come from many reasons. It can be the perfect endeavor because it offers freedom. Artistic freedom, freedom to work at the level that suits your lifestyle, freedom to raise your children without constant daycare and the financial freedom that has come from building a reputable business offering quality products.

There is nothing like being a special part of a community's celebrations by sharing your talents. As trends and tastes change over time, one thing remains constant; cake will always be a part of so many life celebrations.

While this is a great business, it should be noted right up front that there are some challenging aspects to every business – even if you are fortunate enough to live in a location that permits home businesses. The ability to bake tasty and beautiful cakes is not a guarantee of commercial success. Knowing how to decorate cakes and starting a business are two different things.

Like any new start-up, cake decorating does require a commitment of your time, energy and finances. These changes may be an adjustment with which your family may have an initial hesitancy accepting. You will want to discuss all of your plans and have the full support of your family before undertaking this new career. Spouses are particularly important to have on board, wholeheartedly. The last thing you want is someone who disapproves or is bringing negative energy into your business. Coming to an understanding about the realistic expectations of everyone involved—from the children (if you have kids) to the family pets, everyone needs to be aware of the possible changes taking place.

Your family's support is probably the most important factor if you are considering this as a home business. They will be directly affected by your business. As Earlene Moore points out, most birthday parties, special celebrations and weddings are held on the weekends. This may mean that you are not available to your family at all times, during their leisure time. Advance planning and keeping a calendar of events is a must to avoid conflicts during those really important family occasions and commitments. Most successful entrepreneurs will tell you that they never could have made it if their family wasn't 100% supportive. Sure, there will be times when your work gets in the way of family time and this can cause tension, but overall, you want and need a supportive environment. Without it, your business will fail. Here's a great article about balancing your home business and family life: http://www.powerhomebiz.com/vol15/separating.htm

START UP CONSIDERATIONS

HOME BUSINESS: If your municipality permits you to operate from your own home kitchen, the start up costs are much lower than starting a commercial bakery in a rented space. The biggest difference being that you won't have another rent to pay. Still, you will need basic equipment, supplies and extra storage space. These modifications to your home can be disruptive at first. Again, depending upon where you live, you may be permitted to work at home, but not in the family kitchen. In this case, you will be required to meet certain health code requirements for a separate kitchen and entrance for your cake decorating business. You may have to rewire for special equipment, run new plumbing lines for additional sinks, and/or add hot water capacity. The Health Department may have rules such as no pets or children in the preparation and storage area. Other changes to your home may be required as well. The expense of bringing part of your home/kitchen up to code, modifying the décor, getting a license and passing an inspection must be part of your planning, even if working at home.

LEASING: Another option, if you cannot operate from home is to lease a commercial kitchen. Although there is an initial cash outlay, this is a great option for part time cake businesses. Leasing a legal commercial kitchen means that you can bypass the certification and inspection process – this has already been done and is part of what you are paying for. This is a particularly good option if you are just starting out and not sure if you want to make the big investment of buying or building a commercial kitchen, or modifying your home. Moreover, leasing means that you can quickly get into this business, legally. Depending upon the arrangement you make, leasing can also be a money-saver in terms of equipment. Many commercial kitchens for rent provide professional equipment as part of the agreement. The cons of leasing are that not every community has commercial kitchen space readily available. It takes time and energy to find a suitable space. As a starting point, check out:
http://www.commercialkitchenforrent.com/

OK, let's take a look at the many immeasurable benefits in operating a cake business:
- You are the boss! You can take on as much work as you deem appropriate.
- You will incur fewer start-up and overhead expenses in a home business than if starting in a commercial location, but a leased commercial kitchen enables you to make money faster.
- You can raise your children or take care of an elderly person who may need your presence at home if you work at home. Even if you work in a commercial kitchen or standalone shop, you have the flexibility to schedule your life that most people don't.
- You can see prospective customers by appointment only.
- You have greater flexibility to be there for your kids.
- You can work when you feel most productive – be it early morning or late at night.

Of course, as you grow and are in greater demand, the flexibility decreases – this is something you should plan for. If one of the main reasons you're getting into this business is control over your own life and schedule, what will you do when the orders start coming in? How will you meet the customer's expectations as well as the demands and expectations of your family? It is important, up front to ask yourself if you are a disciplined person who can run a business and a life outside of that business. This

START UP CONSIDERATIONS

is the challenge and excitement of building a business that will ensure a great income!

Make a list of pros and cons for yourself. Be very honest about your own personality in terms of motivation, the potential for unusual hours, budget management, organization, occasional uncomfortable customer interactions, and weigh the benefits with the inconveniences. For most people the benefits of owning their own business will far exceed the initial challenges. You're not the first person to do this, so there are many resources on which you can rely. First and foremost, you can find a community of peers online in cake decorating business forums such as cakecentral.com. The internet has made it possible to share information, ideas, recipes, techniques, and most importantly support for cake decorators worldwide. If you're not already participating in such an online community, I urge you to join one immediately. More importantly, participate actively in discussions.

Despite the economic fears we all have, rest assured, this business is light on risk if you start off carefully and PLAN, PLAN, PLAN.

Remember: Even in touch economic times, people celebrate special occasions (and eat cake!)

Wedding commerce alone is a 35 BILLION dollar industry in the United States. Whether you plan to specialize your efforts towards this market or diversify your offerings to include birthdays, catering, restaurant clients or other special events, there is plenty of opportunity for a cake decorating businesses. In the following chapters, everything from design ideas and equipment decisions to building a client base and financial considerations will be explained in detail.

CAKE EDUCATION

CAKE EDUCATION

If you are really serious about cake decorating as a business you must first educate yourself right away. More importantly, you must continually broaden your skill set. Trial and error can be beneficial but it will not prepare you to own a cake decorating business.

Decorating classes teach advanced skills and techniques to streamline your efforts. When you are responsible for delivering a wedding cake, you don't want to be looking up a technique with 24 hours to go. It must come to you with speed and accuracy. Cake decorating classes for the novice decorator, as well as any decorator who wants to increase their skills is the perfect place to get started. You can find cake decorating classes anywhere from a local crafts store, community colleges, cake decorating supply stores, and even private instructors. Classes range from beginning Wilton Method Classes [http://www.wilton.com/classes/classlocator.cfm] all the way up to culinary seminars and courses at the French Culinary Institute [http://www.frenchculinary.com/courses_cpa.htm] There are even camps and cruises dedicated to cake education.[http://www.cakecamp.com/] [http://www.cakecruise.com/].

Gear your class load towards the kinds of cakes you want to make. For example, if you want to use rolled fondant or gum paste techniques in your cakes, you need to take more advanced classes. If you are a beginner, make sure you enroll in a beginning class. Before registering for a beginner class find out exactly what the class offers. Typically this information will be available on the website of the class but you may have to call for clarification. In addition to the basics such as the cost, time and place, you will want to know what specific skills will be taught—especially if there is a specific skill you wish to acquire. You also want to know if students are required to bring their own supplies and on what they will be practicing (real cakes, practice boards, inverted pans, etc.) Finally take the time to learn about the instructor. How long has she been decorating cakes? How long has she been teaching? Often teachers will provide testimonials or referrals from former students. If you are making a significant investment in a cake class, you may wish to ask for referrals from former students. Call them and find out how they liked the class and the instructor. Most people who decide to teach are wonderful communicators and love sharing their gift.

Many cake shop owners, just like you teach more advanced classes and offer practical advice. If you can find them, they are one of the best resources as they tell it like it is! Again, online forums fill this void for many people, who do not have local resources but if you can develop a give and take relationship with someone nearby, all the better. Keep in mind, local cake decorators are ultimately in competition with you to some degree. Approach them with respect, and generosity. Make it clear for example, that if ever you can not complete an order, you would like to refer the business to them. Be forthright about how you expect your services to differ from theirs and never talk negatively about other businesses. It always gets back to them.

Again, if you are a novice, start with this online resource first. [http://www.wilton.com/classes/index.cfm] Wilton is the probably the most popular resource for cake decorators. It is here that you learn the fundamentals. Of course, everyone looks to Wilton as a starting point and that may feel frustrating to you if you're someone who wants to create something more unique. Keep in mind that a strong foundation in the basics will enable you to go anywhere you want creatively when the time comes. Don't get drawn into the latest cake decorating trends before you've mastered the basics as every design relies on a fundamental skill set. Wilton is just a starting point for your initial needs as a cake baker. They are certainly the biggest, but as your business and skills grow, you will find your own unique resources! The internet has opened up so many amazing possibilities and resources that didn't even exist or we're impossible to find just a few years ago.

Aside from the big names like Martha, FoodNetwork and such, here are just a few resources you may want to check out:

http://www.cakecentral.com--Largest Cake Decorating community. Recipes, Photos, Instruction
http://cupcakestakethecake.blogspot.com/ -- Everything Cupcakes: Reviews, articles, news, interviews
http://flickr.com/-- Photography community. See cakes and cupcakes out in the wild. Incredible artistry
http://youtube.com/ Search for cake decorating, cupcakes, how to videos
http://www.cakejournal.com/ --Cake Decorating blog with many How-to's
http://www.cakespy.com/ Articles and reviews
http://thecakelab.com/blog-- How to's and tutorials
http://www.bakerella.blogspot.com/ --Famous for her Cupcake pops, featured on Martha Stewart
http://www.cakedecorating-stuff.blogspot.com/ -- Cool techniques.

There are so many independent blogs now that could take up an entire chapter to list. Start with these and we will add more to the cake-business.com website soon.

SHOPPING RESOURCES
http://www.cakestands.com -- Asymmetrical Cake stands
http://www.beryls.com -- Hard to find British Beryl's Cake Decorating and Pastry Supplies!
http://www.cakesbysam.com-- Award winning decorator, cake decorating supplies for the novice and the professional cake decorator.
http://www.cookscakeandcandy.com -- Cake Decorating and Candy Supplies
http://www.creativecutters.com -- Design and manufacture quality metal gumpaste cutters and tools
http://www.cakedecoco.com --Wedding cake stands
http://www.caketopsplus.com -- Cake toppers, silver cake plateaus, wedding cake toppers
http://www.discountcakedecorating.com -- A great resource. In business since 1968!
http://www.kitchenkrafts.com -- Another great place to get your supplies (wholesale accounts available!)
http://www.petitfleurs.com -- Petitfleurs, gumpaste and sugar flowers

While the internet provides immediate gratification, and often has free resources, books are a constant resource for the cake decorator. When you just want to have it on your bookshelf you may consider starting with these classics as referred by Earlene Moore:

Wilton Publications
Yearbooks: The yearbooks are a constant source for new cake ideas, essential and new equipment and basic instruction.
Encyclopedia (tips & uses) # 3:
This book is an absolute storehouse of basic information. It offers an overview of the tip groups and explains the many things that can be done with each type of tip. For a beginner to a master cake decorator this is a wonderful reference.

START A CAKE BUSINESS TODAY

Winbecklers Books and Videos
The Winbecklers are talented bakery decorators who have written and published several small books and DVD'd. These resources provide wonderful demonstrations of buttercream flowers, figure piping and other cake decorating techniques. They present beautiful work in a style that is oriented towards production work/speed.
http://www.winbeckler.com/

While the Winbecklers books and videos are classics, they are sometimes difficult to obtain in a timely manner from their website. You may find it more efficient to order from Amazon.com

Magazines
American Cake Decorating Magazine:
Mail Box News:

Videos
If you cannot find a cake decorating class where you live, you might consider distance learning online or a video course. Amazon/Barnes and Noble carry several videos you may wish to consider.

Contemporary books
As interest in cake decorating has skyrocketed in the last few years, there have been some amazing new sugar artists to publish.

Cakes to Dream On: A Master Class in Decorating By Colette Peters
The Confetti Cakes Cookbook: Spectacular Cookies, Cakes, and Cupcakes from New York City's Famed Bakery By Elisa Strauss, Christie Matheson
Sweet And Simple Party Cakes By May Clee Cadman
Cake Art: Simplified Step-by-Step Instructions and Illustrated Techniques for the Home Baker to Create Show stopping Cakes and Cupcakes By The Culinary Institute of America

Books about the Business
Professional Baking by Wayne Gisslen (Author) this is an important resource used by professionals.

From the Inside Flap *Looking to raise your baking to the next level? Start with the book the professionals use—Wayne Gisslen's Professional Baking. Named the IACP Cookbook Award Winner for Best Technical/Reference in 2002, Professional Baking is considered the cornerstone of a baker or pastry chef's education. Now updated in a new Fourth Edition, this complete baker's companion will provide everything you need to know to master the craft and art of making breads, pastries, cakes, pies, mousses, and more, and help you learn and practice sugar work and cake decorating skills.*

Increasing your skills still comes down to just one thing. Practice. Books, videos, and websites are great for pointing you in the right direction and helping you avoid costly mistakes. The advice of others helps us feel more comfortable and secure in our efforts, but it is no substitute for doing. As a cake decorator, you much practice to achieve speed, skill and uniformity in your work. You can take classes, watch demos and read all of the books but it still ultimately takes practice. You must be willing to make mistakes, throw things away, and start all over. I know its tough at times but being an expert at coating your cakes, smoothing with a spatula, creating perfect dots, bows, blossoms, rolling out uniform fondant, etc. will save you hours of heartache and earn you many appreciative clients when you're doing it for real.

4

YOUR WHY

Whenever starting something big, time-consuming, or otherwise important, it helps to understand your WHY. That is, Why are you doing this? Take a moment now to write down and preserve your reasons for starting a cake or cupcake business. Knowing your WHY is an often neglected first step in starting a business; yet as you get going, and challenges inevitably arise, you can always return to the foundation of your business, your WHY. Do this now while you are thinking of it. It needn't be a lengthy document or polished for anyone else's reading. Just write freely what comes to you.

You may select this as the venture to undertake for several reasons. Perhaps you love baking, and over the years have become a pretty capable and creative baker. Do you have friends and family that say things like, "Your baking is so good, you should go into business!" when tasting your baked goods? Now is the time to transfer that talent to creating delicious items for the consumer.

Convenience
If your community permits you to legally bake and sell cakes from home, you have the flexibility to schedule your own time and work at your convenience. The nice thing about baking and decorating cakes is that it can be done virtually at any time. You can do just about everything involved with the business within your home except for deliveries and shopping trips. You can use your kitchen oven and many of the cooking utensils you already own. Further, you only need to purchase special equipment, as you need it. For example, if you need a particular baking pan or special ingredients you can wait until the job that pays for their investment.

Minimal Risk
Whether you can use your own home kitchen or you lease a commercial kitchen, there is minimal financial investment in starting a cake or cupcake business compared to so many other alternatives. Unless you modify you home extensively, or renovate another space, you could easy walk away from this business if it wasn't viable for your family or if you simply didn't enjoy it. That is why I encourage many entrepreneurs to start part-time. Educate yourself not only about cake decorating, but also running a business. See if all of the other parts of the business: book-keeping, client interaction, clean-up, maintenance, supply ordering, etc. come to you as naturally as the artistic piece. Keep in mind, everyone has their strengths, and running a business may not be yours. Don't despair; there are resources for helping you in that area as well. We'll talk about them later.

Of course if you offer quality products, and great customer service, your business will grow. Even in difficult economic times, people get married, and in most circumstances, couples always need a wedding cake. There will always be a market for cakes and once you learn how to properly nurture it, you will see your venture take off!

Work at Home MOM
You may be in the situation of wanting to start a home business while "staying at home" with your children. Depending on where you live, this may be an option. Even if the law says you can not work from home, you still can take advantage of the networks you've established as a mom. Your connections

from school, church, little league, etc. are all potential clients. As you network with other families, let them know of your new business. Subtlety is the key here. First and foremost, these are your friends and mixing friendship and business can be a tricky thing. While you want to use your networks as a way to get the word out, you don't want to come across as "taking advantage" of the friendship. Likewise, you don't want your network to feel they are entitled to the infamous "friends and family" discount. I've seen too many times, cake decorators who have to dig themselves out of difficult pricing structures because word got out about special discounts. The problem becomes, who is entitled to a discount and who isn't. Even more troubling is when the friend doesn't realize they are getting a discount and starts telling others about your super low prices. My advice is this: consistency and transparency. Write it down, even if you don't publish it on your website, a policy that states how and when you handle discounts. For example school and church events get a break if you don't have paying customers in the queue. Charity events are pro bono if you have the time, and so forth. The main thing is don't give a big discount to one friend unless you're prepared to field that same request from others. If you have a policy, even if it's informal, you can fall back on it and not feel badly or like you're giving away all of your profits.

With that said, I do think that when you're getting started, there are opportunities to present your products to wide audiences. For example, volunteer to bring one of your cakes or cupcakes to a class party or school function. The teachers, parents and guests will see and taste your work first hand. Teachers in particular are well connected throughout most communities and their endorsement will mean orders for you in no time. If you are ever asked to donate a cake and you wish to do that, I would recommend including an invoice with the cake upon delivery (e.g. taped to the box). The invoice should indicate the total price, as it would be normally, and very clearly indicate the discount. You can explain that it for record keeping purposes – tracking all of your expenses.

Cake Decorating with Children in the House
One of the cons to working at home can be the children. Unless your kids have clear boundaries for what is expected of them when you're working, children can create a hurdle in your workflow. You may need quiet time when decorating a particularly difficult or complex cake design. There might be times when you are learning a new skill and need an uninterrupted hour or two; or there may simply be the need to talk on the phone with a client without someone screaming in the background. The best way to take care of this is preparation. First of all, prepare your kids. Make very clear your expectations of their behavior when you're working. What kinds of activities are OK when mom or dad is working and what things are not OK. That said, we all know it's not simple or easy. Your kids are going to want to be with you when you're home. Often taking a short break for some uninterrupted time with them can save your hours in the long run, if you're constantly being interrupted. You will need to organize your time very well when you have deadlines. Of course, as a stay-at-home mom you already know the importance of time management, but your business may require some additional refinement of that skill. You may consider joining a babysitting co-op or if you live in close proximity to family, they will surely want to support your new business. Taking care of the children for a few hours is the perfect way they can help assure your success.

If you're starting this business to be at home with your children, frequently shipping them off to daycare, babysitters and their grandparents isn't something you will want to do on a regular basis. It is rather a necessary circumstance on those occasional days where your concentration must be at the highest level.

Network with other moms to learn how they do both parenting and a home business. Here's a terrific WAHM resource you should check out if you don't know about it already: http://www.wahm.com/The parents here are great at offering advice that will help you succeed with kids in the house.

YOUR WHY

Part Time

If you are presently working at a regular nine-to-five job and dream of starting a cake or cupcake business, you can easily start your business in your "spare" time. In fact, starting your business this way is a smart option. Your financial risk is minimized because you still have a steady income, and you can determine if you really want to pursue the business full time before you invest significant time and money. Once you're sure your new venture can support you, and you'd had the opportunity to experience the reality of running the business, you can transition the business to full time.

Part time cake decorators often concentrate on providing wedding cakes. They are frequently the most profitable, they are usually scheduled far in advance, and most orders are scheduled for pick-up on Friday or Saturday morning. By preparing in the evenings during weekdays you can do much of the advance work (mixing icing, making decorations, preparing cake boards, etc.) ahead of time. For example, for Friday pick-ups you can bake on Wednesday evening and decorate on Thursday evening. For Saturday pick-ups, bake on Thursday evening and decorate on Friday evening. Pace yourself during these times when you have deadlines at your 9-5 job and make sure you have then energy to do a great job. It can be very challenging at first trying to muster the energy to bake after a long days work. The motivation and adrenaline will be there, but don't burn yourself out. Remember, as Ben and Jerry say…"If it's not fun, why do it!"

The main advantage to starting your business while still working your regular job is the relief from financial pressures. As mentioned previously, it may not pay off for you to stay at your job or even work part time once you reach a certain level of success. But until you know the ebb and flow of the income cycle, it is a big risk to throw everything into this business.

Once you do go full time, your finances might be tight for a short time as you get started and there is always the issue of health insurance if you are not partnered with someone who is covered by health insurance. However, being at home or being ones own boss can be the most urgent concern for many people. Those committed to developing a quality product and service can make it! Remember, many wedding service providers are independent operations that bring in several hundred dollars (and more) per event. With a steady clientele anyone can meet or exceed their financial requirements.

Lifestyle

Of course you don't have to be a stay-at-home mom to do this business. You might be retired and enjoy the additional income as well as the social interaction this kind of business brings. You may be someone who loves your regular job but wants to add this endeavor to your life (and get paid!). For whatever reasons you may have, cake decorating is a business that can be tailored to fit any schedule and any lifestyle. We all know that health insurance is a huge crisis worldwide so approach this issue with caution. It can cost a self-employed family of four, several thousand dollars in health insurance each year. There's no silver bullet answer for this problem for ANY entrepreneur, but because of the crisis, a wide range of information and options are available. An educated consumer is a smart consumer. Use the internet to learn about
- the different types of policies available to you;
- the companies that offer insurance;
- insurance agents and local companies;
- what different policies will pay for and what it won't;
- how you will be reimbursed for your visits, prescriptions, and other medical services

http://www.healthinsurance.org

5

GETTING STARTED

Getting started with birthday cakes is a great way to introduce your business to the community in which you reside. You might also look for business baking cakes for baby and bridal showers. These cakes will be your bread and butter in the beginning, but the wedding industry is where your business can really take off!

Consider, that while birthday and other celebratory cakes are important in their own right, they do not have the same connotation as the all-important wedding cake. For most brides and guests, the cake is a tremendous symbol of the celebration. It is a very large part of a reception, and highly photographed when the wedding couple cuts it. A cake plays a large part in the reception's decoration and is a focus of any buffet, often on a table decorated with the bride and the bridesmaids' bouquets. People at her wedding will discuss the cake, just as they discuss the wedding dress or flowers.

If you are confident in your work, you should start taking orders for wedding cakes immediately. If however, you want to take some time at less pressure-filled opportunities, then consider starting smaller. Very soon after starting your business, you will probably have requests from friends for cakes for any number and type of event. It won't take long before the friends of your friends start calling for their events. And from there, as they say, when it rains, it pours.

If you have been thinking about this business for some time, then you probably already have some great design ideas. Perhaps you've seen cakes that you've admired or even ones you thought were entirely unattractive and said to yourself, "I could do this!" Even if you have the "perfect" cake design, there are some important business considerations that have very little to do with aesthetics. Rather, you need to consider how what you offer –the specific products you sell--effects your profits. Every cake you offer has its own unique set of requirements and thus each cake can take up different resources. You will need to invest in different ingredients and possibly different equipment. Make sure the majority of products you offer are profitable by keeping your selection to a minimum and doing some market research into the most popular products.

Now, I hear you saying "but I want to be unique, one-of-a-kind, custom...." and I agree you should have cakes that set you apart- cakes that distinguish you. But if you want to stay in business you have to have a handful of cakes (or cupcakes) that make most of your profit. You don't have to know what they are when you first open, but in addition to expanding your skills as a cake artist, you should also begin recognizing what kind of cake most of your customers will buy and how much they're willing to pay.

What will you offer that customers will pay a little more for as opposed to buying from the grocery store? What sells in your community? I would urge you not to rely on your own feelings about this, but rather to go out in to the community and learn first hand.

GETTING STARTED

1. Make a list of all of the wedding cake providers in your area. This can be done in many ways: the Yellow Pages, weddingwire.com, Google search ("Wedding cake, Nashville"), yelp.com, etc.
2. Visit them. Check out as many different kinds of cake and cupcake businesses as you can -- even grocery stores, WalMart and Costco. You want to educate yourself about their products and the customers who shop there. You won't be able to visit small home businesses without a commercial storefront, but you can call them and review their website.
3. Make note of the cakes for sale, and if possible, the cakes sold. How many varieties of cake are there? How many fillings? Can you see a trend? The goal in this exercise is to determine the most popular cakes where you live. You can learn this by watching customers and what they purchase, by what the shop is making (if in sight) and by asking, "What are your most popular cakes?" Most cake decorators aren't going to share this information openly as this is a competitive business, but it is certainly not unheard of for a bride to ask a cake shop owner what are the most popular cakes. Sometimes, owners are more than happy to share this information, other times, they won't. It never hurts to try. You can also discover the more popular trends on the Cake Business Forum at cakecentral.com. Keep in mind these may not be local trends though.

Some businesses you may want to visit multiple times others, such as small independent shops, you may want to pay a visit, but do further research via their website. Once you have visited multiple cake businesses you will have a greater insight into what sells in your area. You should be able to identify the cakes that are most in demand and you should undoubtedly include some of these cakes in your own product lineup. Of course you will make them in your own unique flair and artistry, but you want to have the head start of knowing what sells before you generate a completely random menu.

Once you have identified the cakes that are in demand, you will need to perfect the recipes. You may need to tailor your existing recipes to the tastes and expectations of the local community, based on your research. You should also take into consideration, the availability of the ingredients before making any final decision.

There are some cake decorators who are comfortable making any cake based on the request of the customer. While I understand that kind of flexibility will result in more clients in the short-term, it can result in lower profits because you don't control the ingredients. Before you ever agree to take on a cake that you've never made before, be sure to cost it out before quoting a price.

6

MARKETING

Without a doubt, there is a huge market for beautifully decorated custom-made cakes, but in the early stages, most businesses require some degree of marketing to get the word out. The most efficient means of marketing today is a website. Your presence on the web is your public face. It tells prospective customers who you are, where you're located, what you sell, and how much your goods might cost. Most importantly, it enables the customer to see your cakes.

When you're writing the copy for your website, you should think of it as part advertisement, and part information. After visiting your website, you want the bride to take the next step with you, whether that is a phone call, a tasting, or a contract. Your website has to both sell and inform. If you already have a website, pull it up now.

- Does your website explain both the practical (flavors, pricing, dates available) as well as convey the intangible benefits of why a customer should use your services?
- Is it easy to navigate? Can users find images, prices and your contact information with ease?
- Is your web address easy to remember? Have you avoided words in the URL that might easily be mis-spelled?
- Does it load quickly?
- Does your website show up at the top of search engine results for your local community?
- Have you registered your site with Yahoo and Google Local results?
- Is the majority of the site "Above the fold" or do users have to scroll to see everything?
- Are there references from other satisfied brides?
- Do you offer a newsletter, blog or any other ongoing communication with prospective and existing customers?

If you answered "no" to more than a few of these questions, your website might be due for a refresh. In today's world, so much of a bride's research in completed online. You want the experience that represents you online to be as fresh and polished as the product you offer. You've probably heard that marketing your product is the key to success in any food business -- cakes or otherwise. Ask yourself, why would a customer want to buy my product? Your website should help the customer understand these factors. Don't just think about it. Write it down.

In addition to taking the time and effort to really concentrate on your business, to verbalize and document it, building a website is a critical step if you haven't already done so. Most prospective clients will ask for your URL. A website is flexible enough that it can be used in a number of ways. You may wish to work with the media, go to trade shows, contact buyers directly and use it to impress financial backers. A website is part of public relations and will help:

Establish your credibility
Position your cake decorating business as a serious (but fun), high-quality endeavor
Enhance your reputation and grow your client base
Build consumer confidence and trust

MARKETING

Cultivate new markets
Impress financial backers and encourage investors

Business Cards
A low tech but equally important step in marketing your business in a personal and cost effective way is business cards.
Not only should you have them, but also you must carry and hand them out on a regular basis. Carry business cards with you everywhere, and give those cards to everyone with whom you come in contact. Everyone you meet is a potential customer. I used to suggest simple black and white cards, but as this business has become more competitive, you really need to distinguish yourself from the crowd. Invest in color cards, glossy if you can afford it.

Think about the opportunity! How many celebrations have you been to where there wasn't a cake? Talk to everyone you cross paths with during your day. Share your excitement about being a professional cake decorator! Keep it simple and enthusiastic and you will be more effective. This is often called the elevator speech – what you would tell someone about yourself and your business if you only had about 25 seconds (the time it takes you to ride an elevator with a stranger). In your elevator speech you have the opportunity to introduce yourself in memorable fashion, emphasize the benefits of a unique home baked product, and get asked questions about your home business. This is the perfect time to give out your card. Everyone likes to do business with someone they have met and feel they can trust. Be yourself and your sincerity will come through.

Starting a business on a shoestring means marketing through your personal network. One suggestion is to join an internet social network like Facebook.com. This is a powerful tool for discovering and maintaining many personal connections. Social networks are great because often people will invite you to connect and they want to find out about you. Facebook is a great way to passively market your business without being "pushy". Your network of friends can opt-in to your profile and read as much or as little about you and your business as they wish. If that is not your speed, you can start by creating a list of everyone you know-you may be surprised how many people you think of! You will probably have no problem coming up with an initial list of at least one hundred names when you include:

- Your family members - even those whom you see only at weddings and funerals.
- Neighbors - include everyone on the address lists of your neighborhood association, your community pool, or Clubhouse
- Friends from church
- Friends from your former jobs
- Friends from your spouse's job
- Parents of your children's friends - use address lists from school, soccer team, gymnastics, Girl Scouts, Boy Scouts, etc.
- Your college roommate's family, friends, and co-workers
- Social clubs Sports clubs
- Your family's doctors, dentists, orthodontist, etc.
- Your attorney, insurance agent, etc.

Whenever you meet someone new, add him or her to your list.

Letter of Introduction

The next step in letting all of your friends and acquaintances know about your new business is to email them with a link to your website. Many people prefer the formality of a paper letter, but I have come to prefer the opt-in nature of email. It is more effective in that it can be shared with more people with greater ease, it can be saved, stored and recalled, and its effectiveness can be measured almost immediately. If your network is interested in your business, they can chose to learn more by visiting your website, emailing you back, or they can save it for another day when it is more convenient to explore.

Up until recently I might have though this too informal, but almost everyone communicates via email now. In fact, by some standards, email is considered "old fashioned" ☺

Even though you will send the same message to each person on your list, take the time to address each email individually, including each recipient's name at the greeting line (i.e., Dear Judy, not Dear Friends). Don't send out a bulk email with everyone's address in the header.

The following is a sample of an introductory letter that you may use or revise to better fit your business:

Dear Patty:
I am excited to tell you about my new cake decorating business "[Your business name]."
Made from scratch using the freshest ingredients, each cake is a unique work of art and can be decorated for any occasion-birthdays, baby showers, office parties, weddings, etc. I am a small business owner who prides herself on creating an excellent product and providing superior customer service. Delivery is available to your home or office.

When your next special occasion approaches, please call me or visit my website. I would be delighted to create a cake for you and your guests.
Please feel to share this email with anyone you think might be interested. Mention this email and receive 10% off your first order.*
Thank you for your support of my new cake decorating business.

Sincerely
YourNameHere
www.yourURLhere.com

*wedding cakes excluded

Proofread the email multiple times, as it represents you and your business. Invest the appropriate time to ensure your email is totally professional and perfect.

After you send this initial batch emails, continue to add to your list the names and addresses of new friends you meet each day. Personal outreach is critical at this stage of the game. Moreover, it sets you apart from impersonal grocery store bakeries or business too large to connect to the average customer.

Should you decide that a tangible letter is more appropriate for the clientele you wish to attract and the message you wish to convey, follow the above format and keep careful records of all expenses involved in this mailing for tax purposes: cost of paper and envelopes, postage, etc.

Postcards
About 3 months after you've sent the introduction – be it an email or a letter, your next step is to send a postcard. **Note: Anyone who has contacted you via email, whether they have replied to your initial email or have used a form on your website, should be put on a special email list. You should not use the postal service to contact them as this is a duplication of effort, and a waste of money. This group has

indicated that email is their preferred method of contact.

Postcards can be used to remind people of your cake decorating business so that when they have a cake occasion, they will call you. Consider sending out quarterly reminders in the beginning. Once you learn of a customer's birthdays and annual events, you can send them targeted order reminders. Again, this is where social networking tools can be used effectively. Most social networks ask the user to identify their birthday and they can choose to make this information public.

Create your own postcards by purchasing 8-1/2" x 11" card stock and printing four cards on each page. (You'll need a paper cutter or pay a printing service). Your postcards should be different every time you do a mailing. Keep each card simple and quick to read. An example might be:

Your Business Name
Beautiful and Delicious Cakes
For All Occasions
555.777.1234
Delivery Available to Your Home or Office
Visit our website at: www.greatcakestoday.com

Every communication from you—email, mail, every phone call, and every business card that you hand out is one more reminder to a potential customer that you are available for their next cake occasion. Make it your mission to keep your business name and telephone number in front of everyone you meet.

Special Events Facilities
Introduce yourself to special event coordinators at country clubs, colleges, restaurants, churches, and other facilities that host weddings, rehearsal dinners, and other special events. Keep in mind, that over the past few years cake decorating has become so popular (and thus competitive) that the managers of these facilities have become inundated with such introductions. The key to distinguish yourself here is to bring proof of your status as a legal, licensed provider, keep the interaction very brief (shows respect for their time) and leave a business card that stands out from the dozen or so others in her desk. Some facilities have no in-house food service and keep referral lists to share with their clients. Even if they have in-house catering, often bridal and groom's cakes are not included in their repertoire, and, again, they will refer clients to you. Getting business via referral from a special event coordinator is far more likely once you have actually provided a cake at the facility, so anytime you deliver a cake to such a venue, make sure to leave a good impression. If you can establish a good rapport with a coordinator you clearly will have an advantage over competitors who will follow.

Creative Marketing Ideas
Whether your home-based cake decorating business is located in a small town or a large metropolitan area, you can use creative marketing ideas to let people know about your business. Small towns may offer an advantage in some ways, in that you can become a big fish in a small pond. Even if your town is home to someone who has been decorating cakes "forever," if you are savvy, persistent, and consistent in your marketing plan, your business can grow and become well established.

You may live in a large city where large catering companies, storefront bakeries, and home-based cake decorators abound. Do not allow yourself to be intimated by "the competition" -whether it is the little old lady who has been decorating cakes since 1940 or the plethora of decorators found in large cities.

Develop a marketing strategy and work on that strategy every week. The advantage you have may be the top hit in the search engine results or an advertisement on Craigslist.

As you explore various marketing opportunities, you may begin to see a pattern of one or two producing more results than others. You may discover a certain group or a couple of groups of people calling on you more than others. Pay close attention to which marketing strategies work best for you and focus on those strategies. Make note of what type of person the majority of your customers seem to be (i.e., office managers ordering cakes delivered to the office for their monthly employees' birthday party), and increase your advertising to that type of person. You may discover a niche market for you business that will provide a large portion of your orders. Cater to that niche, while continuing to market to other groups.

Some marketing strategies you may want to consider include:

An ad on Craigslist
You can post information about your cake business on craigslist.org in the "services offered" category for free. You will probably attract a younger audience in this venue. Tell your prospective clients about your cake business and provide a link to your website. You can even include photographs and as much contact information as you like.

Google Adwords
For very little money you can set up an ad campaign using Google Adwords to direct a targeted audience to your website. This is particularly effective if your website is not in the top rankings for organic search results. The way this works is, you tell Google how much you're willing to pay for anyone who clicks on your ad. It could be as little as five cents (.05) for certain keywords or keyword combinations. If a bride searches for the keywords you've placed ads against, your ad appears in the sponsored listings. If she clicks, she is redirected to your website and you owe Google a few cents for the referral. You can set a daily budget limit and have an unlimited list of keywords and phrases.

Create an eBay Auction
It might sound crazy, but I've seen many wedding vendors achieve success with this strategy. In the listing, explain the limits of what you're offering such as a maximum number of servings, the timeline under which the buyer must claim their cake, additional charges, etc. Set a reserve price (the minimum amount you will accept) and make sure you're About The Seller page is filled out. Even if no one bids on your auction, eBay is a great marketing tool and their site often shows up very high in Google search results. Visitors to the auction or classified ad, can learn more about you and will want to visit your website.

Ads in Local Newspapers
Create a list of every newspaper within your community and surrounding areas. If you can get a copy of the newspaper, look up the cost of ads. Most small independent newspapers also have websites where you can find out ad costs. A simple classified ad can be inexpensive and sometimes free. When placing an ad, order it to run as long as possible. A one-time ad is not nearly as effective as an ad that readers see over and over again.

Newsletters
When you receive newsletters or learn about a newsletter, find out if they allow ads. Newsletters may reach a smaller group of people, but larger ads in a newsletter can be very inexpensive. Know the target audience of the newsletter before making a decision.

Likewise publish your own electronic newsletter to people who sign up on your website. This might include articles such as wedding cake trends, the pros and cons of fondant, information about your upcoming schedule, customer testimonials, etc. You can use a free HTML form generator from Wufoo[wufoo.com] and manage your contacts via Aweber[Aweber.com], Constant Contact[Constantcontact.com] or simply set up a free gmail account just for this purpose.

Food Editors
Increasingly weblogs have grown to be the ideal place for finding articles about unique small businesses such as yours. You can often garner the interest of a website simply by emailing them and expressing your appreciation for their site and inviting them to share your site with their readers. Likewise, food editors in newspapers may be interested in writing an article about you and your business. Please note, it is important that your business is legal and licensed if you wish to be featured in a newspaper. Health inspectors read too! It would be a shame to generate a lot of buzz around your business only to have it shut down a week later.

Refrigerator Magnets
Turn your business card into a refrigerator magnet. The magnets can be given to each customer when they pick up their cake (along with other "plain" business cards to give to the guests at their party). See: http://www.4imprint.com

Bridal Gown and Tux Shops
Visit bridal gown and tuxedo shops in your area and request permission to display your business cards on their counter top or bulletin board. Purchase inexpensive, clear cardholders in which to display your cards. Ask the shop owner for permission to display a beautifully decorated dummy wedding cake in their store. The display is a lovely and appropriate decoration for their shop and can be combined thematically with their items.

Car Magnet
Make sure your car displays your business information: http://www.magneticsignsontime.com/
or
http://www.iprint.com/

Collaborate and share the expense

Consider collaborating on displays with other wedding providers including:
* rental supply companies
* gift shops,
* florists
* wedding videographer and photographers
* stationers
* musicians

A small tabletop easel would hold a list of each business that provided an item for the display, along with a phone number and website for each.

Other Wedding Vendors
Speak to the owners of other shops in your area that cater to the wedding and special events industry. Ask about placing your business cards in a prominent location in their shops and possibly creating a display similar to the one described above, using their items along with a bridal cake. Also ask about collaborative advertising opportunities. Other businesses to consider include hair salons nail salons, day spas, jewelry stores, etc.

Bridal Shows

Bridal shows are held in many cities throughout the year, but especially January through March after all those Christmas engagements. Consider having a booth or a display at an upcoming bridal show in your area. Bridal shows often include a bridal attire fashion show with lots of door prizes, followed by time for attendees to stroll and check out the booths of businesses catering to the wedding industry.

Consider making a sheet cake and serving a small slice to visitors to your booth. (Ask event organizers how many people attended last years show to estimate your cake size.)

Display at least one dummy wedding cake.
Make sure each booth visitor receives your business card. You should consider giving these items to everyone, not just potential wedding cake customers. As noted before, everyone has a birthday sometime!

Craft Shows

The same bridal show-type set-up can work at a crafts show. You are, of course, not there to sell anything, simply to make contact with potential future customers.

Other Places for Cards and Displays

Below are other businesses and groups that you might consider asking for permission to display business cards:

- Children's party places - gymnastics centers, skating rinks, pottery making stores, etc.
- Places where women gather - scrapbooking stores, gyms, beauty salons, crafts stores, etc. child-care facilities

Online resources.

Make sure your business information is listed in local "free" directories such as:
Google Local Business Center [http://www.google.com/local/add/lookup]
Yahoo Local [http://local.yahoo.com/]

Also, many communities have wedding related websites where vendors can add their business info for free. These information portals often draw brides because of the one-stop shopping aspect. Brides can quickly see what services are available in their community. But remember, they're far more likely to search out a vendor who has a website so get something online ASAP.

NOTES:

7

GET TO WORK

Classes, videos, instruction books and drawing can teach you how to use the tools and certain skills of cake decorating, but nothing prepares you like doing the work! Practice everything. Bake and frost cakes often, master the art of coating your cakes, and lettering them. Practice combining colors, designs and flavors in a pleasing way. Consider sharing your talents through demonstrations and exhibits. After all, if you're going to demonstrate to others, you have to know your stuff!

Equipment and Recommendations
Cake decorating requires specialized tools that are relatively inexpensive. You've probably already had many of these items around your kitchen before ever even exploring the idea of making a business using them. Some tools can wait until you have a specific order that requires their use.

You will need the following if you don't already have them:

A (legal) place to bake.

An oven - This does not have to be a specialty-baking oven though it should be able to regulate the temperature correctly. If your oven is undercooking in one corner and burning in another, it is probably time to head to Sears. If you are just starting out, you may want to consider a small convection oven. It doesn't take up much space and can fit up to 5 standard sheet pans (18"X26" pans) at a time. If you are thinking about professional baking equipment, keep in mind that most large pieces of commercial kitchen equipment can cost upwards of $10,000.

Stand-Up Electric Mixer - An essential piece of equipment for the cake decorator is a powerful stand-up mixer. The KitchenAid 5 or 6 quart stand mixer is perfect for the job. A significant investment, yes, but it will pay for itself in time and labor saved. Shop around for this item because you can often find it on sale, especially around the holidays or a holiday like Mother's Day. Professionals typically use Hobart mixers (they made the original Kitchen Aid mixers years ago). They now make a 5-qt counter top model along with the professional ones. The model number is N-50. Keep in mind, this will set you back about $1500 and you could replace the Kitchen Aid several times over for that price!

Turntable - A turntable is a must for decorating. It provides a stable platform and it helps assure you are decorating equally and evenly. Any turntable will work fine at first, but when you start getting into larger, heavier tiered cakes, you will want to make sure your equipment provides the appropriate support. Invest in the best quality turntable you can afford.

Baking pans - Purchase various sizes as they are needed. Make sure the pans you purchase have 90-degree sides and corners. If you will be doing cheesecakes, purchase pans with removable sides.

Cooling racks- Start with two cooling racks at least 12" wide. Purchase larger racks as your business requires.

Angled spatula - For applying and smoothing icing.

Piping (or pastry) bags - For creating borders and other decorations.

Couviers - For changing tips easily.

Tips - Basic tips include those used for lettering and creating flower petals, leaves, and borders. Purchase others as needed.

Dishwasher – some might say optional, but they certainly save a great deal of time when cleaning (and time is money).

Other Items to remember:
- Greaseproof paper
- Tissue paper
- Foil
- Icing scraper or comb
- Icing ruler or comb
- Serrated knife
- Cake boards
- Decoration for top of cake
- Pillars (if required)

When you are really ready to make a go of cake decorating as a business, you (and if applicable, your spouse) need to determine exactly what you can afford to invest. With a pool of available funds, specifically earmarked for your new business, you will probably have to do some shopping. Typically, aside from the physical space (rent or remodeling, the biggest investment you will need to make is in an electric mixer. Once you complete your research and purchase a mixer, you will probably also realize that there are a host of other wonderful items that could be used in your decorating business.

If you are one of those people who LOVES to shop, be wary of going too far too fast, to purchase much more than you really need. You see, despite all of the wonderful products that are out there, most of your work will be done with a few essential tools. Be steadfast about buying only the tools required for the designs you are offering. That means planning ahead and making some design decisions early on. (You can always change your mind.) Unless a special request comes in from a customer for a custom design, you really won't need anything other than the basics listed above. When you receive unusual requests, you simply make a special purchase, and pass part of that cost along to your client.

Purchasing Pans

When purchasing cake pans, it is advisable to always shop at a professional bakery equipment supply house, craft store, or online cake decorating site rather than a department store. Talk to professional bakers about the pans they use and check out online forums for bakers. If you plan on using your pans for a long time, investing in a quality product makes all the difference. Your spouse may not recognize the difference, but remember the adage, penny wise, pound foolish -- don't skimp on quality products that need to be used over and over again. Because the innovations are always changing, I advise reading the reviews from Cooks illustrated.
[http://www.cooksillustrated.com/] They test everything and weigh the cost versus the durability.

It's a good idea to purchase multiple sets of the basic shapes because a simple 2- layer cake requires 2 pans. The speed of your workflow is greatly enhanced if you don't have to stop, wash and refill a pan for another layer. As your business grows you will want even more sets, but try to purchase specialty pans as they are needed for specific cake orders. The standard sizes you will work with are 5", 6", 7", 8",9",10",14" and half rounds for larger sizes such as 18" & 22" in order to fit in your oven. Additionally, half round pans also allow proper air circulation, and the cake bakes more evenly than in an extra-large round pan.

8

BUSINESS

Simple but Important Ideas for ANY Entrepreneur

Keeping Overhead Low
This is a difficult heading because ultimately, "low" is a relative term. There is no way around spending money when you're developing a new business. It is the equipment and ingredients that you buy that will help shape your business.

While there are ways of cutting corners, the small investments still can add up quickly.
1. Offer an internship with a local high school student
2. Buy only the items you need when you need them
3. Use your home telephone line instead of a business line
4. Print your stationary and invoices
5. Partner with other like businesses
6. Use an extra room in your home as an office

#1: Offer an internship with a local high school student:
Many high schools and technical centers offer culinary arts programs and/or agribusiness classes. You can get great assistance from students who are looking for experience or are required to have real work apprenticeships as graduation requirements. Students can help with numerous production needs, and can grow into loyal employees with the proper treatment and respect. Avoid college students who are near graduation or grad students if possible. This is your competition in 12-24 months. While I don't fault them for trying, I wouldn't hire them. They are trying to get experience, ideas and recipes that they will later use in their cake businesses in your community.

#2: Buy only the items you need, when you need them :
This has already been discussed, but it's important so here it is again. It's easy to get caught up in the excitement of having new things. Even when a business is well established, owners often desire to have the latest equipment. That is why advertisers have jobs. They know how to make the consumer's mouths' water with desire for their new offerings. It is a good idea to exercise restraint when you have some money available for buying equipment. Buy only the equipment and ingredients for the orders that have been placed. If you have a strong track record and can adequately predict demand, then order in bulk. Build up your equipment inventory slowly. The fastest way to go out of business is to buy too much equipment or have ingredients spoil. Perhaps you're thinking of a chest freezer or a commercial grade oven. Sure, these are great to have, but wait until your business really takes off! Some equipment may sound critical – a must have; but when it comes down to it, the equipment isn't always a necessity. Additionally this point refers back to your product offerings. If you offer too many cake options that aren't profitable, you'll have too many ingredients on hand. Maintaining a proper cash flow is so important to running a successful business.

#3 Use your home telephone line
When you're first getting started, there may be no need to spend money on setting up a dedicated phone line. Unless there are others at home during business hours, an additional line may be a luxury that can wait. If, however, you have children who might tie up the phone you may want to invest in a business

line, cell phone or Skype account. If you decide to maintain only one line a simple solution is to simply answer the phone by saying your first name so whether a business or personal call comes in, you're just saying hello in a nice, but professional way. Also, check out Grandcentral.com. This application enables you to provide a business phone number that rings into your home or cell phone.

#4 Partner with other like businesses
Building a relationship with a complementary business such as a caterer, wedding consultant, etc. is a delicate matter and certainly an option that does not come without much work, research and discussion. In fact, it isn't for everyone because it can involve building financial ties with other businesses – not easy or always wise when you're starting. Such an association can however help you develop some very good sales opportunities without ever investing money in advertising. If you do wish to join forces with another company, be sure to be careful when affiliating yourself before doing extensive research. Get to know everyone involved. How will you work together? What will be the financial issues involved? What if you are bringing in more customers than your partners? Discuss these things up front and consult with professional, legal representation.

#5 Home office. No rent. Great tax benefits. Contact your accountant or IRS.

Advertising

If your budget permits the investment, you can reach your audience via paid advertising. Google Adwords is an inexpensive option to start. While free options have been discussed previously, there are paid options that will enable you to reach a broader audience. I recommend that any paid advertising you consider drive local traffic to your business. While it might be impressive to have an ad on theknot.com, take into consideration how much local business such a placement will bring in. You will be better served through advertisements in your local print media and establishing working relationships with wedding businesses frequented by your potential client base. Advertising enables you to highlight your quality products to a wide range of people in your area.

The best way to reach your target audience for cakes is through the wedding-related services they use. As mentioned above, you should establish working relationships with businesses such as tuxedo and bridal gown shops, wedding photographers/ videographers, jewelers, event coordinators, caterers, ballroom/special event location managers. Another strong networking opportunity is available through your local area chamber of commerce.

If you decide to start investing in advertising, a great way to begin is by talking with similar businesses to find out where they advertise. Here is a great reason to be on collegial terms with complementary businesses. Other more experienced businesses can share with you their good advertising investments and help you avoid wasting money on ineffective ad placement.

Once you determine the best places to advertise within your budget, you may need some help writing/designing the copy. The best way to learn how to write ads is to read ads. Of course you wouldn't copy them word-for-word, but use well-written copy as a guide to writing your own. As you get a sense of commonly used wording and style, you'll be writing effective ad copy in no time.

One important thing to try to keep in mind is to always highlight benefits as opposed to features. The difference is critical. For example, "Our cakes are made from scratch from only the finest ingredients" is a feature. "You can rest assured your guests will be delighted with the exquisite confection that is your one-of-a-kind cake." is a benefit. While the feature (made from scratch, finest ingredients) conveys the means, the more important benefit to the bride is that she can have confidence in what she's serving her guests. Most good advertising conveys more benefits than features.

Take note of this strategy sometime when you find a convincing ad that you like. A great exercise in preparation of writing your own copy is to make a list in two columns. On one side, write the features. On the other, the corresponding benefit. This will help you distinguish between the two.

When selecting a publication, be sure it is appropriate to the product you are offering. To invest your advertising budget wisely, do not overlook the publication's circulation and demographics. When you get serious about investing your advertising dollars you should pre-qualify the publication you choose by going to their offices and asking questions regarding their market. Usually the advertising department will have an in-depth analysis of their consumers so you know to whom you're selling. One way of pre-qualifying the publication is to contact the businesses that advertise and ask them about their results.

Study the publication to see what other kinds of services are being advertised and how.(i.e. classifieds, small black and white ads, text only, 4-color photos, etc.) Keep in mind that these publications often write featured articles and they prefer to write about the businesses who advertise in their publication.

Again, contacting other business can establish potential networking opportunities. You'll be surprised how much free publicity you can get just from corresponding, calling and networking with others.

You may be able to pool advertising dollars for joint advertisements. A great example is a cake decorator and a photographer and caterer. As long as each respective business has a similar sense of style and are priced in appropriate proportion to one another, joint advertising can be a great way to save and build relationships. It is to their benefit as much as it is to yours.

If advertising in more than one publication, be sure to ask your potential clients how they found you. Thus, you can determine which ads are working. Keep a record of every ad you place. Depending on the kind of publication in which you will be placing an ad, you may or may not need a professional designer. When first getting started, it may not be high on your priority list to invest in professional design services. If you decide to work with a designer, be sure to discuss upfront issues such as deadlines, their fees for making changes, submission fees, etc. Some designers offer a fee for a turnkey service—from concept to publisher, while others charge ala-carte style for every service they provide.

Record the date your ad is sent to the publisher and the date you received a checking copy, proving that your ad appeared. Some publications require you to sign a contract while others have less formal agreements. Particularly when purchasing a series of advertisements, you'll want to keep good records of when the ad is due to appear, when it appeared, and if applicable, the terms of agreement for the ads placement (location) in the publication.

While the trend is shifting to the internet, many brides still refer to the yellow pages when starting out. Getting a listing in the yellow pages is still an important step in promoting your business to your surrounding geographical area. The yellow pages while quickly becoming outdated are still a resource for many brides when they are starting their search for a cake (wedding or otherwise). They yellow pages know that they must compete with the internet so they have begun offering web-based services to compliment their paper distribution. Keep in mind that and every year more and more people who grew up not using yellow pages will become consumers who prefer to do their searching online.

In most cases, a profitable business occurs when word-of-mouth advertising takes off, so placing multiple ads may not be worth the added expense. Select the channel or publication, be it the internet, the yellow pages, the free community magazine or the newspaper that goes to the widest population and includes an urban area (if applicable to you). When placing an ad anywhere, be advised that often sales representatives work on commission and may try to sell you a space larger than you need. Unless you live in a large urban area, advertising for cake decorator businesses will not be so oversaturated with ads so that one stands out more than the rest. In fact you may have the only ad in some publications. Advertising is important, but don't worry about it immediately. Concentrate on the free publicity you can get from newspapers, websites, and community newsletters.

Accepting Credit Cards

Accepting credit cards is a convenience many professional businesses offer. The main benefit is that when a bride wants to book a date, you can take the non-refundable deposit right over the phone (unlike a check that you must wait for). The downside is the expense and fees associated with every transaction. There is a wide range of services out there, so do some investigation. Ask other businesses who they use. You'll want to compare rates and fees. Potential costs include: set-up charges, installation fees equipment rental, and transaction charges. All merchant accounts vary, so shop around and ask to have all options explained to you. There are online merchant accounts as well, though their transaction fees tend to be higher. Before you set-up a merchant account you will need to:

Open a business account with a local bank: This is as simple as putting money into the bank. To open up a business account you will need to visit the customer service representative at your local bank and tell them that you would like to open a business account for your business. If you are the only employee of your company, you will open your account as a sole-proprietor. A sole proprietor account is very simple and you can use your social security number for tax purposes. If you have a partner, you will need to have that person accompany you to open your business account and you will file taxes as a partnership. If you plan on having employees then you should contact a professional tax advisor immediately.

Contact a Credit Card Processor. Your bank may offer credit card processing. Should you decide their rates and service are acceptable to you, it is very convenient to keep all of your accounts with one bank.

Customer Service

What will you do when a mistake happens? Create a policy in writing to inform your customers of your excellent satisfaction guarantee. For example, explain your policy if you make an error. For extreme errors, offer the choice of a partial refund, complimentary items or a credit for free cake in the future. Of course individual circumstances require individual solutions, but it is a good idea to let customers and potential customers know you respect the adage; "the customer is always right," and that you will fix any problems that arise.

The key to minimizing costly errors is documenting everything—every conversation, every agreement should be written down. Great customer service is the key to a successful business. A positive demeanor, quick response to customer concerns and friendly service in all situations are critical. The way you protect your business however is explicit clarity on every detail, e.g. the cake design, the flavors, the servings, the proper cutting method, the extra costs, the delivery fee, the return of rentals, etc. Each of these details can be included in a contract or agreement signed by both parties. When the father of the bride calls up with buyer's remorse a week after the wedding, complaining about some "mistake" you've made, you can refer to the contract signed by a responsible party. Additionally, you've captured a digital photograph of your cake upon delivery so the documentation of a successful installation protects you from any mistakes made by employees of the reception venue. At all times be courteous, inquisitive and respectful. If you've made an honest mistake, own up to it, offer the proper remuneration and move on.

Word gets around quickly when an owner/operator is difficult to work with. In the same vein, word also gets around when a store has not only great products, but also friendly service. When it is a real pleasure to do business with you. Your customers will return to you more frequently and refer new people to you. Having a policy in writing makes it all the more real to the client thinking about writing you a check for several hundred dollars.

Insurance

At least two types of insurance will be needed for your home business. If you are able to work at home, your equipment may be insured for its full value by adding a rider to your existing homeowner's/renter's policy. Your insurance provider will advise you on the appropriate amount to carry as an additional umbrella policy to cover liability. If your are starting as a part-time business, disability, health, and life insurance may already be in place through the your primary place of employment.

Whether you work at home or if you rent a commercial kitchen, you should also carry Product Liability insurance. This protects you in case a customer claims your cake harmed them. This may seem excessive and unlikely, however, lawsuits are common in our society. Even claims that are invalid can move forward in today's court system. If you don't carry Product Liability Insurance, and someone decides to sue you, your business and personal savings are at risk. This policy can cost upwards of $1000 a year, but it is worth the piece of mind.

As your business expands to a full-time endeavor, health insurance coverage may continue in place as part of your benefits. As the business expands, the issue of benefits may be evaluated based on the needs of the qualified staff added to the company.

The types of coverage you should discuss with your agent include:

General Liability and Product Liability—will cover the bodily injury of another person or their damaged property arising out of the owner's negligence. General liability also covers things like a customer taking a fall over your front steps and twisting an ankle, or you breaking something during a delivery. Discuss with your agent the scenario of someone being injured/becoming sick from your products.

Business Interruption—is vital for the full-time business owner who faces not only a loss of income, but also the ability to keep up with operating expenses as a result of a catastrophe. This policy will cover expenses such as rent, salaries and utilities.

Workers Compensation—is for the business owner who employs a staff of one or more persons. Mandatory in most states, it provides coverage for medical care, disability income benefits, death benefits and rehabilitation services.

Setting Up Your Office

When getting started with a cake decorating business, there are so many things to remember and so many documents to keep track of. Be sure to set aside space in your home office in addition to your kitchen, specifically for the business. The tax advantages of a home office may be significant. A cake decorating business doesn't a storefront, at least in the early stages. As you grow, you may want to consider that route.

A home office does not have to be glamorous, but it does need to be exclusively used for business. The IRS typically looks at home office deductions very carefully and you may want to consult with a tax advisor regarding such deductions.

Taxes/IRS

Your company will be established as a sole proprietorship (unless you plan to have partners). You can usually file your business taxes under your personal 1040 using your Social Security number as the business tax ID.

Whether you work entirely from home or rent a commercial kitchen there are many potential tax benefits to running part of the business from home. (e.g. billing, phone consultations, supply ordering). Ultimately, you should contact professional tax advisor. A percentage of your home expenses is deductible when you use a percentage of your home exclusively for the business. In rare situation where you are using your kitchen both for your business and for your personal use, you will break down this percentage even further. Your tax advisor will help you calculate this figure.

Your deductions may also include all ingredients, equipment, and utilities such as electricity, water, gas as well as any renovation costs for your work space (if you at home) or rent and mileage (if you lease a commercial kitchen). Don't forget about services such as garbage removal, maintenance and repairs. Travel and auto expenses are deductible when the travel is specifically business related. Internet expenses, office supplies, advertising, business meals, cake related books (including this one), equipment repair, and many other items are deductions you may be able to take. If you rent, the same deductions apply when you pay for them directly. The most important thing is to keep excellent records and receipts of ALL your spending.

If you try to remember expenses months after the fact, you will spend far more time tracking down receipts and probably will make errors. You can simply keep all receipts in a box even if you can't get to the bookkeeping right away.

Record Keeping Tip:
You may want to get a business-only credit card. Having a credit card for your business means that if you make a purchase and forget to document it immediately, you have both a monthly and year-end statement to remind you. Your gasoline purchases for example, don't get mixed in with personal use and you don't have to keep track of hundreds of little slips of paper receipts. Usually your statements are available online. This is particularly useful if you lose a paper statement. Your statements can usually be downloaded into business bookkeeping software like Quickbooks.

Mileage Records
Record the mileage and drive time to each place that you deliver a cake for future reference and scheduling your time. The easiest way to do this is a small notebook you keep in the glove compartment. If delivery is in a large city, you may want to include the time of day of each delivery along with the drive time. A 15-minute drive at 1 p.m. may take more than an hour at 5:30 p.m.! Take your mileage records with you when meeting with your income tax professional. Your advisor will probably tell you that delivery mileage is tax deductible, unless you charge for delivery. Other mileage, such as business-related shopping or consultations are typically tax deductible.

Business or Hobby
It is very important to the IRS that your business in not a hobby. Even if you have another job, your cake decorating business is likely entitled to tax breaks if you are running it as a business. The IRS considers

a hobby an activity "carried on for personal pleasure or recreation." The considerations for being identified as a business include: the activity being carried on in a "business-like" manner; enough time invested into your efforts to demonstrate that you intend to make a profit; you depend on the income for your living; your losses are beyond your control (start-up losses are normal); you make changes to make the business profitable; you or your advisors know what they're doing to make the business successful; you've made a profit in similar activities in the past; you start making a profit eventually; you can expect to make a future profit from the appreciation of the assets used in the activity. All of these qualifications do not need to be met to qualify as a business.

If you are making a profit, another important consideration is the self-employment tax you will owe in addition to your regular income tax. The self-employment taxes pay for Social Security coverage. If you have a salaried job covered by Social Security, the self-employment tax only applies to the amount of your home-business income that, when applied to your salary reaches the current ceiling. State taxes and potentially sales taxes apply as well. Again, talk to a pro.

The website www.irs.gov has a wealth of information regarding small businesses.

Name Your Business

Deciding on business name is often one of the first things people think about when starting their business. Your business name is part of your brand identity. Deciding upon a name is not a simple decision to make, because your business name will establish potential clients' first impressions of you. Taking the time to investigate the successful and unsuccessful names of other companies is an often-neglected first step. In today's age of Internet searches, it is also important to select a business name that can be translated to a .com. Even if you're not planning an immediate foray onto the web, reserving the name you wish to use is a prudent step. You should check with [http://www.register.com] or [godaddy.com] to see if the name you like or some derivation of it, is still available for Internet registry. (1and1.com is also a great place to register your domain name and host your website— not only for their low prices but for the free services they provide.)

You want customers to remember you, so be creative. Because of the nature of a cake decorating business, you can really play with words to generate something unique. While you would never want to copy a name that already exists, check out some of the names of Cake Decorating businesses online. There are delightful examples that may help you brainstorm.

Again, with a creative name, you will more quickly establish name recognition for your businesses. When naming your business, you may also want to avoid selecting a personal name, like Rachael's Homemade Cakes. While you may have lovely name, it may get lost in the sea of other businesses. (This is not a steadfast rule, particularly if you can integrate it into a creative theme.) Try to be really innovative. Also avoid names too closely related to existing businesses. This can result is legal problems, if another similarly-named business feels you are impinging on their trademark.

Be sure to ask the advice of family and friends for their thoughts on your business name. Brainstorming always works better in groups and with people you can trust.

Picture Your Image

When starting a new business your logo --like your name -- gives the important first impression of who you are. It must look professional. I recommend hiring a graphic designer to do this work for you. Fortunately, there are many resources that can make this cost effective. The internet enables you to draw from a huge pool of talent and thus more people are competing for your graphic design business. The result is higher quality work, more choices and lower costs. Here are a few websites you should consider for your design needs:

- 99 Designs [http://99designs.com/]
- Elance [http://www.elance.com]
- LogoBee [http://www.logobee.com]
- 50Dollar Logos [http://www.50dollarlogos.com/]

Once you have created a logo, it should be placed on all materials: labels, order forms, signs, tags, business cards, brochures, stickers, etc. Your logo is key to product recognition. Some people respond to words while many others respond to images. Even if a customer can't remember the name, they'll remember the logo. Again be creative.

For ease, create a black and white logo that can be printed in a variety of colors, made into a rubber stamp, printed on a black and white printer, etc. Check out the online service, iPrint [www.iPrint.com] for your printed materials.

When evaluating designs keep in mind that the logo:
- Looks good on print materials (business card, letterhead, invoices) as well as your website
- Could be made into a sign
- Should be delivered in Vector format as well as layered .psd (Photoshop document) and .jpg
- Is easy to distinguish from your competitors

Keeping Track of Paperwork

In today's computer age, many people store most of their documents electronically. This is increasingly easier, more convenient and efficient for small businesses. There is specialized software for bookkeeping, recipe and ingredient tracking and project management (little reminders to keep you on your toes!) [cakeboss.com]. Email is a great way to keep in touch with clients; contracts can be drafted and quickly altered in Word or Google Documents, and financial analysis is simple with spreadsheets.

Most small businesses use computers in some aspect of their business. However relying solely on one technology to keep track of everything is not the best way for everyone, particularly the "technologically challenged" or techphobic. Having a hard copy of important paperwork is advisable for every business and the following list identifies the most important paperwork you should keep in easily accessible files or notebooks:

Contracts and Orders

Each contract or order form and its accompanying paperwork should be in a notebook. Even though the document may be computer generated, you might have additional notes, photos, magazine clippings, etc. that need to be "attached" to the contract. Typically we still write on and sign contracts in ink rather than produce everything electronically. It is far easier and more time efficient to keep contracts in a notebook or file, than scanning and attaching electronically. Use tabbed divider pages, include ordering party's name and delivery/pick-up date on the tab of each divider page. (Include dates because you will eventually file other orders from the same client.)

Reference

This file contains your business license and information related legal documents. If someone comes into your shop requiring a legal document, you want to have instant access. These documents, you may want to scan back-ups as they often need to be send electronically to others.

Also keep a file for all business-related receipts. If you shop online, create a screen capture and/or print any electronic receipts and include in this file. Online purchases are easy to forget if you don't keep hard copies. Having a business-only credit card is a failsafe as the credit card company maintains your transactions.

Design Ideas

Most people keep their design ideas in two places –the internet, and a paper file. Increasingly, this is shifting to the web, but brides still love to sort through magazines, tearing out design ideas; so don't abandon the notebook of design ideas yet. This file is a supplement to your library of cake design books. The notebook contains ink jet photographs of your own cakes, clippings of designs from magazines, and an index of design ideas.

Clippings/Recipes

Likewise, computer-based recipe collections are taking the place of recipe notebooks, but I often like to refer to paper recipes in the kitchen so I don't have to worry about my computer. This ebook has hundreds of recipes, but you may prefer the ease of a notebook/cookbook, not a computer screen, when you're ready to try one in your kitchen. As this section of your notebook grows, it can be subdivided into sections similar to the index headings listed below. The clippings should be of recipes that you are confident can accurately duplicate and that would sell well.

A recipe index is the first thing one should look at when discussing products with a client by telephone. Here is where software like CakeBoss can be a great help. You can have electronic versions of your recipes that you can sort by ingredient. This is a great convenience. When you hit upon any product that sounds appealing to the client, you can quickly print the recipe and describe all of the ingredients in detail.

You should also have a file that includes the paper trail from any and all marketing efforts for your business. Include copies of fliers, brochures, sales letters, business cards (yours and clients), all responses to your marketing; records of telephone conversations (include name, company name, telephone number, day of conversation, and content of conversation etc.

9

LEGAL

Every community has regulatory requirements. Some are more restrictive than others when it comes to operating a cake business. Each state has websites to help you weed through permits, licenses and regulations. You may also want to contact your local WBC, SBDC or SCORE office for one-on-one help.

US Small Business Administration Offices [http://www.sba.gov/regions/states.html]

Local WBC finder [http://www.onlinewbc.gov/wbc.pdf]
Local SBDC finder [http://www.sba.gov/sbdc/sbdcnear.html]
Local SCORE Office – [http://www.score.org/findscore/index.html]

Checklist for Small Businesses:

Employer's Identification Number (EIN). Obtain an employer's ID number with Form SS-4, if you have employees, are a partnership or are incorporated. Sole proprietorships can also obtain and use a TIN instead of the owner's social security number on all business forms that ask for a "taxpayer identification number." If a business is not a corporation this identification or Social Security number will be needed before a bank account can be opened.

Obtain a federal license if required by federal law. Employers must obtain licenses, which are renewable every two years.

Probably your business will be a sole proprietorship. However if you grow or have business partners you need to determine the legal form of your business. Are you incorporated, a limited liability company, or are you establishing a partnership?

If needed, obtain seller's permit - also known as Certificate of Authority or Resale Certificate. Get a resale tax certification or state sellers permit if the operation will involve purchasing items for resale. This exempts the business from paying sales tax on some of its purchases. Handy when you buy items in bulk! Keep excellent records though so the IRS doesn't think your taking advantage of this.

Obtain any trademarks, if needed. Trademarks are words, names, illustrations, or a combination of these used to identify products or services to distinguish them from items of other firms. Check with the Trademark

Register of the United States to avoid using trademarks already used.

Obtain any required state licenses. Most states issue licenses to a business that will provide food services.

Obtain occupational or health permits often required for food preparation.
Acquire zoning approval, if necessary. Zoning ordinances regulate how property can be used. These

31

ordinances are tools of both state and local governments to regulate the safety, structure and appearance of the community. Make sure that the zoning rules in your area allow the operation of your kind of business.

Obtain a local business license. Many municipalities or states require a permit to conduct business. The fee is usually based on gross sales, but volume from most part-time ventures falls below the minimum tax level, so, at least initially, it won't be costly.

Register your business name if using a name other than your own or a variation of your name. Check with the county clerk locally, and the secretary of state nationwide to determine if a certain name is legally clear.

Know the Law

Many factors should be considered if you decide to explore the possibilities of making foods other than cakes at home. It is possible that your town does not require a separate commercial kitchen for cake decorators, but does require separate facilities for other types of catering. Additional licenses, rules, and regulations may apply as well.

If you are only doing a couple of birthday cakes a week - the expenses of having a legal baking facility will not be practical for you. If however, your business grows enough for you to be viewed by regulatory government offices as a "real" business, Earlene Moore shares the fundamental of what may be required based on her experience of getting legal in her small community.
[http://www.earlenescakes.com/business03.htm]

Check with your local Health Department for the requirements to have a legal health inspected food facility in your town. Each state and town has different requirements. Some states are very lenient with small home baking businesses and only require you meet standards when you surpass pre-determined limits. Other community governments simply ignore you, until you are so big you'd need a larger facility anyway. If you happen to be in a city with a very strict health department - you must meet health and other regulatory standards or risk being fined.

The risks are real. What happens is a legal bakery will turn you in because they don't want the competition. Some counties start a fine for illegal food preparation and sales at $350-$500 for the first offence. The second offense is usually double ($1000) and the third offense is double that ($2000). It's hardly worth the risk for most cake decorators.

The following is a list of things that may be required of your home baking environment to become a legal business in the eyes of the government. It changes from state to state, community to community. The lists are only offered as a guide. The addendum of this book provides the contact information and the regulating body for every state.

> 3 compartment sink with a grease trap installed
> Hand sink
> Lights covered (They make clear plastic tubes that cover the fluorescent bulbs)
> Washable surfaces - walls, floors, cabinets, counter tops
> Ceiling must be of non-absorbent material

Separate refrigerator, freezer, oven (with thermometers)
Separate Entrance
Storage for Equipment - pans, spatulas, bowls, etc.
No pets in work area
Approved Water source
All Ingredient containers must have covers and be labeled in refrigerators, freezers and cabinets
Heating and Air Conditioning may need to be separate from the house system.
If your cake decorating area is to be a separate building from your house you will probably be required to have a small rest room
Check your zoning laws to see if signs are allowed for your business in a residential area.

Legal Record Keeping

Records must be kept for tax and legal situations:

Receipts for all cake related expenses (Ingredients, classes and etc.)

Mileage on Car – any driving related to your business.

Utilities records - gas and electricity that you use in baking and decorating should be deductible on your taxes. A percentage is usually used - depending on the volume of cakes and the size of your work area.

Cake order records - Keep your cake order records for your protection and reference. Protect yourself and keep those records for a sufficient period of time. It is best to consult your tax advisor for the time for which you should hold onto records. An efficient way to do this is to scan your records and save to CD. They also work great as a reference when a new bride wants a cake just like her best friend. You may not remember what the other bride ordered, but you can pull her order and you can find the flavor, design and have all of the specifics in hand.

Licenses --- never open a business before checking WITH AN ATTORNEY. Most home decorators make the mistake of growing a significant business without a license of any kind. While laws vary between states, counties and cities, ignorance is never an excuse. There are basically 4 areas you must comply with when setting up a business:

o Heath department --- county - or city. Ask them for a list of regulations.

o Building & zoning --- will the area where you want to open a business be zoned for business or is it strictly residential?

o Department of agriculture --- you must be inspected by them whether you live.

o Vendor's license. This allows you to collect sales tax and pay it to the state. See: http://www.taxsites.com/state.html

This may sound scary but it is really quite simple. You call your State Department of Taxes and them that you are opening a cake decorating business. They may have more detailed questions for you, and then within a week or so, tax forms are mailed to you. You fill them out, reporting taxable sales, and send them with your check each month. Some areas also require a 'business license.' Look no farther than the United States Small Business Administration: http://www.sba.gov/ or your local county government website.

NOTES:

FOOD SAFETY

To be successful in any food related business, one must produce items that are safe and wholesome. The production of safe foods is your responsibility. Time and temperature abuse of foods contaminated with food-borne pathogens will certainly lead to a food-borne outbreak that would likely destroy your reputation and business. If anyone gets sick after eating your cake you may also find doctors bills or worse, a lawsuit on your hands. These problems can be avoided if you follow safe food handling practices.

- Purchase high-quality foods from a reliable vendor. The food should be in good condition with the packaging intact, fresh (not beyond expiration date), and at the proper temperature.
- Store potentially hazardous foods, such as eggs and milk, immediately in the refrigerator (33 to 40°F).
- Dry staples should be stored at 50 to 70°F.
- Practice First-in-First-Out (FIFO) to insure safety and quality of your items.
- Ideally, frozen foods should be thawed in the refrigerator 18 to 24 hours prior to preparation. However, thawing under cold running water (<70°F), in the microwave, or extending the cooking time are all acceptable methods for thawing food
- Practice good personal hygiene when preparing and handling food. Wash hands before food preparation, after handling raw foods, after using the restroom or at any time the hands become soiled.
- Take measures to prevent cross-contamination of food if you cook your family's meals in the same space where you bake and decorate cakes.
- Clean and sanitize food contact surfaces such as counter tops, cutting boards, equipment and utensils. One tablespoon of bleach per gallon of water is an effective sanitizing agent.
- Wash fresh fruit thoroughly under cold running water. In refrigerator storage, make sure fresh fruits are wrapped or stored in containers separately from raw meats.
- Wear clean clothes and aprons when preparing food.
- Do not use the same towel to wipe food contact surfaces that you use for wiping hands.
- Clean storage and kitchen areas regularly.
- Practice good housekeeping and implement a pest control program for eliminating the spread of disease.

Many jurisdictions require that you have a Food Manager's Certificate to make food for pubic consumption. This might also be called a Food Safety or Food Sanitation permit. The regulating health agency in your community wants to make sure you're educated in proper sanitary practices.

An example of a food safety program is ServSafe offered by the National Restaurant Association Educational Foundation. Their website provides state-by-state regulations and guidance. [http://www.servsafe.com/Foodsafety/]

SELECTING RECIPES

One of the most important decisions you will make in your cake decorating business is the selection of your cake recipes. As you first begin cake decorating, a good place to practice is on your family and neighbors. Neighbors are very important to you when you decide that this will be a home business. As part of your preparatory stages, conduct a taste test. It does not need to be an expensive one: call your friends and give samples to your neighbors. Try to get as many people to sample your product. Have a list of questions ready. The results can help you evaluate the best aspects of your cakes and designs. This kind of survey can also help you determine what kind of products everyday people are looking for and if there's sufficient demand for the kind of product you bake.

Cake Ingredients
When choosing a recipe, keep in mind some practical maters. Consider the list of ingredients:

- Are all of the ingredients readily available from your supplier?
- Are the ingredients affordable?
- Is your recipe traditional enough yet unique?
- Is your recipe profitable based on what you know about the going prices in your community?
- Is the recipe too complex and time consuming?
- Does the recipe require folding, stirring, or other time-consuming hand-mixing methods?

The dump and mix method is the most cost effective as it consists of only one step: Combine all ingredients in the mixing bowl and mix. Many bakers make good quality recipes by using this procedure.

Keep it simple and cost efficient.
When choosing recipes you may be tempted to start out with extravagant recipes. Be advised that most brides prefer either chocolate, white cake or spice/carrot cake. (Lemon is also popular in the summer)

Build your business around two simple recipes, as they will account for a huge percentage of your orders. Add other recipes when and if the demand exists. The three basic recipes you should consider using should include very simple ingredients and be quick and easy to prepare.

Icing Recipes
You will also want to test icing recipes. Buttercream, royal, and rolled fondant are three basic types of icing that you will want to include in your repertoire.

Buttercream can be used to coat and decorate cakes. Royal icing is used mainly for decorations and rolled fondant is used to coat cakes that are already coated with a glaze or buttercream. Rolled fondant may also be used to create borders, flowers, and other decorations,

Buttercream:
When testing buttercream recipes, use unsalted buffer, not margarine. If the recipe calls for shortening, use the best quality shortening available and try substituting butter for at least a portion of the shortening. Try a variety of flavorings in your buttercream: pure vanilla, almond, and lemon. Keep in mind the health code restrictions you're operating under when selecting recipes.

Royal Icing:

Royal icing is a very basic recipe which is included in containers of meringue powder, one of the main ingredients of this icing. It is important to use meringue powder rather than egg whites in this uncooked recipe to avoid the potential threat of salmonella. The other two ingredients in royal icing are water and confectioner's sugar.

Rolled Fondant:

Rolled fondant creates a flawless, marble-like surface to cakes. It is a bit more time consuming to prepare and is best when prepared at least 8 hours in advance. It must be cooked, kneaded, allowed to rest, and then rolled out like a piecrust before carefully placing on the perfectly smooth cake surface. It is not easy to work with buy yields incredible results with practice. Much of the excitement around cake decorating in the last 5 years has been around the sculptural results that fondant enables. Many brides are concerned about the taste of fondant and need to be educated on fondant best practices. Some people object to the taste of fondant, but others think it tastes great! Fondant is a good option for outdoor weddings in the heat as it holds up better in summer heat than buttercream.

You may want to try the commercial brands of rolled fondant that are already prepared and ready to use. The savings in time and labor would be well worth it if you can find a product that tastes great. Fondant gives the cake porcelain like finish. Fondant tastes a bit like marshmallow, but it is not as soft. When using fondant, don't take a very cold cake into a warm room too soon or it can "weep" moisture.

Fondant should be placed on a cake that is covered with a very smooth coating of buttercream or a smooth glaze. You can use a buttercream undercoat, and use a fruit glaze as well. Another option is to use buttercream between the layers and glaze the outside surfaces before applying the rolled fondant. Inexpensive, store-brand apricot jam makes an excellent glaze.

Here is a simple glaze recipe:

Spoon the glaze over the perfectly trimmed cake, then place the fondant on the cake. Trim rolled fondant at the edges of the cake with a pizza cutter.
The fondant 'scraps' may be used to create borders and decorations.

Apricot Glaze
Ingredients:
30g apricot jam
3-4 tbsp water
a squeeze of lemon juice
Method: Put the jam and water in a non-stick pan, over gentle heat, until the jam dissolves.
Add lemon juice and strain the mixture. Return the mixture to the saucepan and bring to a quick boil, then simmer until it turns syrup.

12

BUSINESS BAKING

The recipes most bakeries use most frequently cannot be duplicated using any commercial mix or combination of mix and "from scratch." If you are uncomfortable using mixes in your business, find recipes that are almost as quick and simple to prepare as a mix. Depending on the volume of business you're doing and the scale of your pans you may need to upscale your recipes. Consult Professional Baking by Wayne Gisslen for detailed explanation of how to do this correctly. You can also find commercial recipes similar your own kitchen recipes and do a little experimentation to perfect them.

When baking from scratch, follow these tips:

Mixing:
- Have all tools, equipment, and pre-measured ingredients needed on the counter.
- You don't want to waste time running around for ingredients, so make sure you have everything on hand.
- Keep ingredients at room temperature for best results. Eggs should only be left out about 30 minutes before using them.
- Scoop shortening from can to the measuring cup with a rubber scraper or spatula. Press it into the cup and level it off with the same spatula.
- Spray baking pans with non-stick product.
- When measuring flour, heap desired amount into measuring cup and scrape off the excess—do not pound or settle it.
- Sift flour, baking soda, baking powder, and spices to avoid lumps
- Mix chopped nuts, dried fruit, or other additions with a little of the flour used in the recipe to keep them from sinking to the bottom as they bake.
- Test your baking powder or soda to see if it still has leavening power by adding a small amount to a bit of very hot water. If it bubbles and fizzes, then it's still good.
- Err on the side of under- mixing-don't over-mix.
- Double check to make sure you did not leave out an ingredient.

Baking
Before mixing batter, preheat the oven, prepare cake pans, and move oven rack to center position.
Try a No-Stick Spray and follow with a light dusting of flour for greasing cake pans.
Place cake pans at least 1 inch apart from each other and from the oven walls. This allows air to circulate.
[http://www.youtube.com/watch?v=6CLZniBlEn8]

Frosting
Crumb coat: to seal in crumbs, spread a thin layer of frosting on the cake, and then refrigerate it. When the base coat of frosting is hard, spread on a final, heavier layer.

A seemingly simple decorating skill that can become very frustrating to a new cake decorator is the process of coating a cake smoothly. Thanks to the internet there are many useful tutorials demonstrating this process. Practice makes perfect.

http://youtube.com/watch?v=iqvL4zhVbE8
http://youtube.com/watch?v=sQgSatRiEHY&feature=related

For a smooth-frosted surface, use a straight-edged metal spatula to spread icing.

Decorating
There are just so many excellent resources for decorating ideas, many of which have been named previously. When you're at your local bookstore you will find those books that provide complete decorating instructions to aid your own work. They will serve as inspiration and as tutorials and they're tax deductible.

This book focuses on the business side-rather than the artistic side---of the cake decorating business. However,
this chapter offers a few decorating tips which are simple enough for a beginner-yet remain favorites of many experienced decorators and their clients.

Cake Preparation
In order to create a flawless icing surface, the cake must be properly prepared. For a comprehensive overview of this process check out the tutorials at [http://www.baking911.com].

1. Test cake before removing from oven. You can test to see if the cake is done by inserting a toothpick, wooden skewer or cake tester into the cake. (Insert tester in several spots, especially when baking large cakes). If it comes out clean or with only a few small crumbs on it, the cake is done. If not, put it back in the oven for another 4-5 minutes.

2. Remove cake pan from oven and place on cooling rack for about 10-15 minutes before removing from pan.

3. To remove cake from pan, place a second cooling rack on top of the cake pan. Securely grasp both bottom and top racks and quickly flip the cake.

4. Carefully remove pan. (If cake is "stuck" to the pan, place in warm oven for a couple of minutes and try again.)

5. Place cooling rack on cake and quickly flip again. The cake is now in the same position it was in the oven. Allow to cool completely before proceeding to next step.

6. Many cakes come out of the oven with a "hump" which must be trimmed to level the cake. Use a long, thin, serrated knife to carefully slice away the hump. Some cakes may not have much of a hump but have a very crusty top, particularly pound cakes. All crust must be carefully removed.

7. Once your cake layer is cooled, leveled, and trimmed, place a dab of icing on the center of your prepared cake board. Flip the cake board over and place it on the cake layer. Place one hand underneath the board or cooling rack and one hand on top of the cake board. Press your hands together slightly and quickly flip the cake.

8. Now that the cake is on the board, make sure the cake is perfectly centered.

9. Next, place the cake on a turntable and ice the top of the layer. If you prefer to add a filling between

layers, pipe a "dam" of icing all the way around the outer edge of the top surface, then spread your filling in the center of the cake layer.

10. Place the next layer that has been leveled and trimmed on a cake board. Cakes smaller than 10" can usually be placed on the lower layer by hand. Larger cakes should not be moved by hand to avoid cracking or falling apart. Use the following method for larger cakes: Make sure one edge of the layer is overhanging the board slightly. Place the board just over the top surface of the bottom layer, allowing the overhanging edge of the new layer to touch the edge of the bottom layer. Holding the new layer steady, carefully pull cake board from underneath the new layer, allowing it to rest on the bottom layer. If you are working on a really large cake and afraid the cake will break when transferring it, you can slip the layers onto a board and freeze solid. Then, assemble the cake using them straight from the freezer. They'll be much easier to handle. If you plan on using this technique, consider the time it takes to freeze when in relation to your schedule and deadline.

11. When the new layer is in place, adjust as needed to ensure that the sides are perfectly in line.

12. Put a small amount of buttercream in a separate bowl. This icing will be used to crumb-coat the cake. Spread a thin coating of icing on top and sides of cake. The icing will probably be very "crumby looking" and you might see crumbs in the small bowl of buttercream. Do not add any leftover icing from the small bowl back into the larger bowl of icing.

13. Wait about 15 minutes for a crust to form on the crumb coating, (you may place in the refrigerator) and then apply the first coat of icing. The icing consistency should be soft peaks, not stiff.

14. Place a large mound of icing on top of cake. Using an angled or bent spatula, begin gently spreading the icing towards the sides of the cake to cover the top.

15. IMPORTANT TIP: When removing spatula from icing, move spatula in toward the center and lift. If you remove the spatula at the edge of the icing, you may pick up crumbs.

16. As the icing begins to cover the top, some icing may extend over the edges. Use that icing to cover sides, adding more as needed. When adding icing to the cake surface, less is more. Add a bit, spread smoothly, and add more as needed.

17. When cake is completely coated, run hot water over spatula and smooth the surfaces with the warm spatula. It's OK if a tiny bit of hot water touches buttercream icing; the water will evaporate.

18. Add at least one more coating to create a smooth, flawless surface.
[http://www.youtube.com/watch?v=5gJZ75ahfs8]

19. QUICK TIP: Try using an "icer" tip to quickly apply icing to cake surface and smooth with spatula. You can also use a Viva paper towel (no pattern or quilting) to achieve a perfectly smooth finish.
[http://www.cakecentral.com/article10-How-To-Create-Faux-Fondant-The-Paper-Towel-Method.html]

Swags

When piping swags onto sides of cake, create guidelines by pressing the rim of a cup or bowl against cake side. A very simple, pretty swag can be created using a #18 star tip. Follow the guideline, zigzagging as you go, and squeezing the piping bag a bit more firmly at the bottom of the swag than at each end.

Another simple technique using dots:
[http://www.youtube.com/watch?v=KuD3vYpIEgg]

Leaf Design
Another very simple, yet very impressive design is the overlapping leaf design. This design is lovely in all white on a bridal cake. Coat the cake with white buttercream icing, then select a #70 leaf tip. Begin at a point at the bottom edge-down at the cake board. Pipe a row of leaves all the way around the bottom of the cake. When you have completed a row, begin the next row just above the first. Touch the base of the leaf to the cake and pull out slightly to overlap the rows. Continue adding overlapping rows of leaves around the entire surface of the cake sides. Add overlapping circles of leaves to cover the top surface, starting at the outside and moving toward the center. When all surfaces are covered, use a smaller leaf tip to fill in any "gaps" and to create another dimension to the surface. You can pull this smaller tip straight out from the surface to create a "stand-up" leaf. Add these tiny leaves here and there all over the cake for a nice texture. The perfect finishing touch for this cake is live flowers. First, wrap the entire stem of each flower with florist's tape, using white tape if you used white icing. (Never place bare stems on or into a cake.)

Cover any surface that will be touched with flowers with cut parchment paper. Place flowers on the center of the top surface or begin off-center on the top surface and arrange flowers in a cascading design down the side of the cake, all the way to the cake board. The leaf design takes some time and may be considered tedious by some, but it is really very simple to do and looks fabulous!

NOTE: Many flowers and plant material are poisonous or have been sprayed with toxic chemicals. Although your contract should state that you are not responsible for flowers provided by the florist, you should be aware of some of the more common poisonous flowers. Several Internet websites include lists of poisonous plant materials.
See:[http://www.cakeconnection.com/freshflower.htm]

Traditional Basketweave Design
See: [http://www.youtube.com/watch?v=X6DryH9o_GE]

A basketweave design is very popular for wedding cakes. Various sizes of tips can be used, as well as combinations of tips. A very lovely look can be achieved using one tip, #18. To decorate the sides, begin by piping a vertical line straight down from the top edge to the bottom. Next, pipe a 1/2" horizontal line over the vertical line at the bottom. Continue piping 1/2" horizontal lines all the way up the vertical line, leaving space in between each horizontal line that equals the width of the tip opening. Next, pipe another vertical line from top to bottom, letting it barely touch the right ends of the vertical piping. Repeat the 1/2" horizontal lines all the way up the new vertical line, filling in the "spaces" created when you left space the width of the tip opening. Continue the same all the way around the cake. The top surface can be decorated in the same fashion. Use the same tip to pipe bottom and top shell borders.

The basketweave design looks very complicated, and the instructions above may sound complicated. The best way to learn how really simple this technique is, is to analyze it by drawing the design on a piece of paper. Don't worry about exact measurements when you draw; just draw it so that you can understand how the vertical and horizontal lines fit together to create the basketweave pattern. Watch the video, as you re-read the above instructions-it will all make sense!

The Cake Board as a Design Element
Don't forget to incorporate the cake board into your overall design. Cover the cake board with a fabric chosen to coordinate with the cake design. Consider using fabrics as the inspiration for the cake design.

After covering the board with fabric and securing it on the underside with tape, cover the board again with crystal-clear cellophane. Buy the heaviest, most durable cellophane possible to avoid tearing when slicing the cake. The finishing touch is a length of narrow, color-coordinated ribbon glued to the side edges of the board.

Silk and Live Flowers
A simply coated cake becomes beautiful when decorated with exquisite silk flowers and touches of greenery. You can get silk flowers from Michael's or order them from:
http://www.somethingspectacular.com/ [http://www.annieandcompany.com]
Flowers and greenery can be purchased in bunches and each flower or leaf group separated using wire clippers. Wrap the stems with florists tape before placing on cake.
[http://www.freshroses.com/] is a great resource for, you guessed it, fresh roses.
Live flowers also look gorgeous on special occasion cakes. Be sure to wrap the stems completely, and, of course, use flowers that are safe.

When planning bridal cake designs using live flowers, you should suggest to the bride that the wedding florist (rather than you) provide live flowers for the bridal cake. This ensures continuity in the overall look of the reception. The wedding cake flowers will be the same or coordinate with the flowers used in the bridal and bridesmaids' bouquets. You may prefer to arrange the flowers on the cake yourself or have the florist do the arranging. Make sure these details are listed in the cake contract. You may also want to give the florist a call a few days before the wedding to confirm cake and flower delivery times, as well as make sure there is no misunderstanding about who will arrange the flowers on the cake. You should also confirm with the florist (not necessarily the person who answers the phone) that no toxic flowers will be used on your cake.

Ribbons
Ribbons can be beautiful cake decorations. In order to place a ribbon on a cake, you tie florist's wire to the base of the bow, loop, streamer, etc. wrap the wire with florist's tape, and place it on cake.

Colors and themes
When working with a bride or wedding coordinator, ask her to bring in any items such as napkins, flowers or color swatches that will be used as a theme in the wedding/reception. You will want to match the colors as closely as possible.

Purchased Sugar Decorations
Royal icing flowers and other icing decorations can be purchased at cake decorating stores or online. These flowers are a time-saving product for many cake decorators and can be effective if used sparingly.

Search local cake decorating and crafts stores, catalogs, and websites to discover the wide range of decorative elements available for your cakes. A starting point is: [http://www.sugarcraft.com/]

NOTES:

13

PORTFOLIO

Your cake decorating portfolio is your most valuable marketing tool. It should contain photographs of the cakes you have made and want prospective customers to see. Your portfolio should exist both as a tangible book of photographs that you can review in person and in digital form on your website. Because cakes only exist for a short time before they are consumed, the photographs in your portfolio are typically the only way for a potential client to see your work. The exception is if a client has been to a reception or other event where your cake is served.

The internet has become the primary way brides (and consumers in general) are reviewing vendors. Big, clear photos – including multiple views- are probably the most important element in determining whether a potential customer goes to the next step with you, whether that is a call, a consultation or a purchase. Even if you're not in business yet or if you don't have a website, documenting your work with photographs is a skill you should always strive to improve.

When photographing your cakes or cupcakes, shoot a tight close-up at an angle that emphasizes the top, but includes the side of the cake as well. Then shoot second and third shots, slightly varying the distance between the cake surface and the camera with each shot.

Your photos have to take the place of your customer seeing the cake in person, so make sure they can see it well enough on their computer screen. Try to frame the shot so nothing else is visible in the frame. If you're shooting at home, look for neutral backgrounds. Avoid situations where there is something in the background such as a child's toy, a dishwasher, dirty pans, etc. This makes your work look unprofessional.

The best way to improve your photography skills is to look at the photographs of others. I'm often reviewing the cake images at flickr.com to see the total range of photographic skill. You do not have to be an accomplished photographer to produce photos for your portfolio. The important thing is that your clients will be able to see a clear representation of your work.

Take a look at photos you've recently taken of your cakes. How do they look? Do they show the necessary detail? Are they clear? Are there any distractions in the frame? Are they well lit? Is there too much flash so that you can't see the details?

The more photos you have of a cake, and the better they look, the more likely you will have a new client when she looks at your portfolio. A trend I've noticed online for displaying cake photographs is the use of blogs. I know it seems like yet another thing to keep track of, but I find it quite effective to see the cake and a brief description or story about the couple who ordered it. Maybe express a congratulatory message or write about a particularly lovely detail in the design. Blogging your cakes gives the impression of how busy you are and it shows the progression from one week to another of your work. See Anne Heap's Pink Cake Box Blog for an example [http://blog.pinkcakebox.com/]

You should begin immediately taking photos of each and every cake you decorate-even fake cakes and practice cakes. The wedding cake is usually photographed for the bride by a professional wedding photographer. You can sometime make arrangements with the photographer to get at least one great print for your portfolio, but more often than not, its not really worth the trouble or expense if you've documented the cake yourself.

Website

Having a website is a must. It is the single most important marketing tool you have other than word of mouth. It is on 24 hours a day. It provides the convenience and detail that brides are seeking and it enables clients to contact you even when you're not available.

A website and word of mouth marketing go hand-in-hand. Consider this scenario: Someone at a wedding or party sees and tastes your beautiful and delicious cake and says: "Who made the cake?"

The hostess replies, "Oh, a lovely shop called ...."Cake By Jane"... This is the perfect word of mouth opportunity that you're looking for right? The problem is, the hostess at this point is typically serving the cake or helping someone find a drink or something else that will prevent her from giving the interested party one of the business cards you've left in the bottom of the cake box.(hint...hint, leave business cards with everyone.)

So the opportunity is missed. Or is it? Perhaps she has memorized your phone number! No, I doubt it.

The easiest way to pass along your information to any interested person, in a format that most people can remember, is a website address, right?

Now, let's replay the scenario from before:

Someone at a wedding or party sees and tastes your beautiful and delicious cake and says: "Who made the cake?"

The hostess replies, "Oh, a lovely shop called ...."Cake By Jane" its: "www cake by jane dot com"...

You're one step closer to a new client! Even if she can't remember the exact URL, the prospect can do a search for you as long as you have a website that is properly formatted to come up in search engine results.

People are far more likely to remember a website than a name and phone number. Moreover, people are much more likely to remember something short and snappy or something very distinct and catchy.

I've found this to be a marketing tool many cake and cupcake businesses and aspiring entrepreneurs give very low priority-- either there's no time left to work on the website or the cost seems too great or they just aren't comfortable with the technology involved.

How to set up your own website:

There are many options for setting up a website:
Free Tools: (*advanced features require payment)

Weebly [weebly.com] Weebly provides you with a free website offering drag and drop functionality for building your pages. They've designed the application to produce sites that are very search engine friendly and have a very contemporary, polished look. I would avoid some of the free website tools that are very outdated looking and where the resulting URL's give an unprofessional appearance. You can have your own domain name: (e.g. www.cakesandcupcakes.com) and still use the free Weebly service. There is an annual charge of about $10. to register and apply a custom domain name to your site.

Wordpress and Blogger.com
Wordpress and Blogger are blogging platforms. They are great for communicating with your clients and colleagues informally. I prefer the wordpress format because it can be transformed into a Content Management System for a more formal website. This means that even though there is blogging back-end (where you post content) the public facing side can look just like a traditional website. Rather than creating "posts" in Wordpress, you create "pages." Wordpress has a WYSIWYG ("What you see is what you get") interface so that you can add the content with no knowledge of HTML. Finally, Wordpress has added a gallery feature to its editor, so you can easily upload and post your cake images in a gridded gallery style interface. We offer a free Wordpress site at [http://www.cakeportfolio.com] if you don't have a website yet.

There are **other Free Website** applications you may consider and I will update the cake-business.com website as I discover more:

Jimdo[http://www.jimdo.com/]
Synthasite [http://www.Synthasite.com/]

Again, I would not use sites like freewebs.com or myspace.com.

If you don't have the expertise to set up a website, consider hiring a small website hosting company or use an outsourcing service to set one up for you. Explain your business and tell them you want to set up a "gallery" of your cake photographs. This does not need to be a fully functional e-commerce site, where you would interact with the client, or process orders. (At least not in the beginning!) As with the logo example mentioned previously, there are many talented designers and programmers in the US and worldwide who can assist you with this. Sites such as Elance [http://www.elance.com], 99designs [http://99designs.com], Odesk [http://www.odesk.com/] and others enable you to shop around for the team that fits your budget. There are many safeguards in place to ensure your transaction is safe. Most importantly, you don't pay until you're satisfied with the work.

Your site should be an electronic version of your portfolio. This is not an expensive site to design or set up and if you are somewhat computer savvy, you could even set up your own.

Your site should include the following:
A home page: The home page should NOT be a flash splash screen that users have to click to enter. In fact, I discourage the use of any flash at all. This is primarily because search engines have trouble with it and your site may not show up in a prominent location. The home page should immediately show the visitor a sense of your style and artistry – whether that is by showing a photo of one cake or several, I will leave up to you. I prefer designs that are uncluttered and simple, enabling your work to show through. The name and address of your business, and easy to find contact information must also be immediately visible. Some brides may want to call you right away and you don't want them to have to search or link to another page to find your contact information.

Navigation on your site should be very simple, easy to read links. Stylized buttons and cute naming conventions are not a good idea. Navigation should be "Global" – that means every page has the same links to navigate to every page on the site. Your links should include the following links: Home, Prices,

Cakes, and Contact Us.

I tend to ignore links such as About Us and FAQ. If you feel you need separate pages to provide special information about yourself such as training or background about what makes you unique then you may want to have an "About Us" or "About Me." If you have many particular details about your policies or questions that you want to answer, then "FAQ" may also be necessary. Avoid putting questions about pricing in the FAQ though. Pricing policies and details should be on the pricing page.

There are many bells and whistles you can put on a website such as Live Support, Newsletter Signups, Google Maps, etc. I would hesitate to put these items on your site at first. You want your site to help the user do what she came there to do:

Look at your cakes, your prices, and contact information. Anything else can distract her from her objective. A blog, however is a great place to share your personality and enable visitors to learn more about you. As long as you have the discipline to keep it up, a blog can be a wonderful compliment to your site. If however, you post a few times, and it becomes idle, an inactive blog can give the appearance that your business is unfocussed. Being busy with cake orders, I'm afraid is no excuse. So approach blogging cautiously. One tip, if you do decide to blog, is to write multiple posts on a day when you have lots of time, then postdate them to appear a few days apart. It looks like you're writing every few days.

If you are not a photographer, a digital camera is the way to go these days as you can insure you capture your cake artistry. Further, a digital photograph enables you to easily repurpose your photographs for your website or physical portfolio. The great thing about digital cameras is you know instantly when you've captured a good shot. You do not have to be an accomplished photographer to produce photos for your portfolio. The important thing is that your clients will be able to see a representation of your work. It is very important to potential clients to see photographs of your cakes. Don't forget to capture detail shots as well as full cake images.

Photographic Setting

The ideal setting for your photograph is usually the reception. The perfect time to photograph the cake is after the other decorations have been set up, but prior to the reception. Timing doesn't always allow for photographing the cake upon delivery, so arrange with the photographer to capture professional shots. If the client picks up the cake you will, of course, photograph the cake in your own kitchen. Upload them to your website or make prints for your portfolio as soon as possible.

Composition of the Photograph

Train yourself to notice the background and eliminate anything that distracts from the cake. Neutral backgrounds are preferred. When photographing cakes at home, try these tips to improve the overall composition of your final print: Place the cake on a sturdy table with a covering that coordinates with (or at least does not distract from) the cake colors and theme. If possible, use the table covering as a backdrop as well. To do this, place the cloth on the table so that the front edge is just below what will be the bottom of the photograph-just out of sight when viewed through the camera lens. Use the back edge of the tablecloth as a backdrop. The goal is to see only the table covering/backdrop and cake when looking through the camera lens.

Make sure the cake is well lighted, whether from natural light, artificial light, or a combination of both sources of lighting.

ALWAYS KEEP A DIGITAL CAMERA HANDY: Make sure you have extra batteries and an extra memory card. Use nothing less than a 5MP or 6MP camera. You can even get a good 10MP camera for $150 -

START A CAKE BUSINESS TODAY

$200. You want high quality shots and 5 megapixels will assure a good resolution. Each year it seems the quality you can get from a consumer camera increases. If you ever forget to take a picture, ask the client if they would please send you a copy of any photo that includes the cake. They are always happy to do so if you've provided good customer service.

***It's Deductible!

Photographing your cakes is an essential part of your business. Therefore, consult your tax advisor about the deducting related expenses, such as the camera, ink jet printer and ink (if printing at home), photo album, supplies and of course, your website.

NOTES:

14

PRICING

Pricing is the most sought after information for new cake decorators. Unfortunately, there is no easy answer and it is probably the most common area for mistakes. **Most new business owners price their cakes too low**. There are a few reasons for this: Often new business owners are trying to compete with illegal home bakers and DIY'ers . Secondly, new business owners lack confidence. They think that because they are new to the market, they can't compete with established businesses, and so they undercut themselves and their competition. This is a classic mistake, especially for those who work from home or are young. Finally, many cake decorators have been baking informally as a hobby for years so charging people feels foreign to them. They're worried about hurting relationships.

Like anything else that causes your business to suffer, write it down. Write down your policy for pricing, discounts, pro-bono work or making anything outside of the normal ordering process. Even if you don't share this information publically you know what your policy is and you can rely on it no matter who asks you. One tip for your social interactions is to never bring the cake that you make in your shop. Rather, make a pie or cookies. You simply explain to your friends that cakes are your business and when getting together socially, you prefer to try something different. That way you put your business in a different category and there is no confusion about the value of your work.

Determining a Price
The big question seems to be: "How do I decide what to charge?" When you first begin in this business you will need to keep your prices competitive with your local competition. Check out what the bakeries and other specialty cake decorators in your area are charging. NEVER, NEVER, NEVER under price the local commercial bakeries. As you gain skills and improve the taste and textures in your cakes you can begin to raise those prices accordingly. The reason people are coming to you for a specialty cake is because they want a product that is better or technique that the bakeries are not willing to do.

Call various grocery stores and bakeries to get an idea of their prices. You do not need to "pretend" that you are going to place an order or even that you are a potential customer. Simply say that you are "calling to find out your price on…" and name the item(s). Websites have made it much easier to do a competitive pricing analysis. Review the websites of other cake decorators in your area. Document the prices per serving on a variety of items such as:

- Birthday cake
- Wedding cake,
- A sculptural cake
- A large sheet cake: Again, note specific dimensions and type of decorating included in the quoted price.

Make sure you are clear about the size of the cake in inches and how many layers. Some decorators have a flat rate per serving, others add on for special details and lots of handworked items. You may need to call for specific details if they are not available on the website. In particular you want to know what sort of decorating they will do for the price they quote.

- A wedding cake with "basketweave" or a "wedding cake with white icing roses and swags on the sides."
- Ask if they do "wedding cakes with rolled fondant icing."
- Ask if they do custom designs or in particular the kind of design you plan to specialize in.

It is not advisable to ask one baker about all five items listed above. Plan on calling as many bakers as possible. Ask on the business forum at cakecentral.com for members (in your geographic area) to share what they're charging for their work.

When you have a good representation of several bakers' prices, begin calculating your costs to determine your own prices. Use the ingredient amounts in your popular cake and icing recipes to determine the actual ingredients cost of each cake. There are software programs that simplify this process and are well worth the investment. The leading application is CakeBoss [http://www.cakeboss.com] Add the cost of cardboard rounds, Masonite or plywood cake base boards, fabric, tape, glue, ribbon, dowels, tips, etc.

A general rule of thumb used by many cake decorators and caterers is to figure all costs of ingredients and supplies, then multiply by three to determine a minimum cost. In the United States, as elsewhere, cake prices vary from town to town, city to city, state to state. Thoroughly research the prices in your area to determine a price that will be within reason compared to others in your area and a price that will be profitable to you.

In the early days of your cake decorating career, you may find that each cake takes more time to decorate than you anticipated. Don't try to calculate your "hourly rate" in the early stages, or you could become very depressed! Remember to give yourself plenty of time to decorate your first cakes. Your hourly rate will eventually catch up with your expectations.

As your reputation grows, you will find yourself filling several orders simultaneously, thereby increasing your hourly rate because preparation and clean-up time account for at last half of your time. When your orders begin to multiply, your speed will have increased as well due to your increased experience. Remember your higher price is not simply because the grocery bakery does a much higher volume of business, but because you offer a superior product and personal service.

DO NOT QUOTE BY SLICES
You may calculate the cake price "by the slice," but always quote a "cake price." A useful price list (which no one ever sees!) lists each cake at a "per slice" rate (for easy calculation) and a "cake rate" for quick quotes. Those "per slice" prices could range from $1.00 to $15+ per slice. This is important because you don't want someone to compare the price of a very simple cake to a very time consuming cake and assume they are the same price.

Using Design and Price Lists
A design and price list is "for your eyes only" - not for public distribution. This list is simply a reference for your use when discussing design options and taking orders from customers. Many orders are received via telephone, so you will simply pull the list and refer to it as you speak with the client. On occasions where orders are taken "in person" - usually at a wedding cake consultation-be discreet in your use of the list. NEVER quote prices away from your office, on-the-fly, or in a rush. This can be an expensive lesson if you do. Additionally, never provide a quote for a lavish, Ace of Cakes, Colette Peters, etc. masterpiece without having an honest exchange, educating the bride about the limitations and expectations of cakes that they've seen in books and on television. A cake like this could take up hundreds of hours of your time, preventing you from taking on any other clients during the same time. Make sure you are compensated appropriately and that the bride does not expect an exact replica.

PRICING

Your design and price list should include:
- The name of the cake design

This is simply a label you give your designs so that you can look up the design on this list. You may or may not choose to refer to this "name" when speaking to your clients about the design.

- Number of Servings

The number of servings from any cake, any size can be calculated by figuring the following serving sizes:

Standard serving size for two-layer cakes is 2" x 1 " x 4"
Standard serving size for one-layer cakes is 2" x 2" x 2"

When mentioning yields of servings to a customer, always tell them the size of servings. If they prefer larger servings for their guests, more cake must be ordered. When discussing wedding cake yields, ask the bride if she plans to save the top tier to serve at her first anniversary or if she plans to serve the top tier to her wedding guests.

- Price Per Serving

This information is for your use in calculating the total cake price for any configuration of tier sizes. NEVER quote a "per serving" price to a customer. Quotes to customers should be for the total cost of the cake.

- Dimensions

You may choose to list several options of dimensions for each design for quick reference. When discussing size of cake with a client, avoid the terms "sheet cake," "half sheet," or "quarter sheet." If you ask a dozen cake decorators the dimensions of a sheet cake, you will get several different answers.

If a customer requests a "sheet cake," offer options by referring to the size of the pan (i.e., 9" x 13" 11" x 15", 12"x l8") and how many servings each yields. When discussing size of cake, always talk "inches." You may refer to a sheet cake as a "one-layer, 12" x 18" cake." A birthday cake may be referred to as a "two-layer, 10" round cake."

- Cake Price

List the total "cake price" for various sizes of your most popular standard designs. This allows you to give a quick quote on some cakes without going through the "per slice" calculation.

- Options
  - Type of Icing

Include prices for various icing options. A buttercream price will usually be more economical than the price for rolled fondant. Many cake designs can be created with either type of icing; some designs are exclusively created with a particular icing type
  - Filling Options

List filling prices as a "per slice" figure for easy calculation.

15

CAKE CONSULTATIONS

Wedding cake consultations are sometimes conducted totally by phone and sometimes face-to-face in your home or shop. Sometimes the bride or her mother has visited your website and will request more information (prices) via email or phone. If your designs and prices seem to fit the bill, your potential clients will want meet with you in person to discuss their cake. When setting the appointment for a consultation, ask the bride to bring any photographs or magazine clippings, sketches, etc—whatever is needed to communicate what her wedding is in her mind. Often she will have provided a link to a cake she's found online.

You will be reviewing all the details, decorations, and colors. Ask her to also bring any fabric swatches (or even paint chips) if she wants color in her cake design. If she already bought a cake topper or other ornaments for her cake, she should bring them as well.

Cake tastings are not required but in most areas they are expected in some form or another. Tastings are a tradition. Brides are getting excited about their impending nuptials and many liked to be catered to. This is a great opportunity to impart the intangible sense of trust – that is, the client can determine if they can trust you with this part of their celebration. The customer service you provide here will often be the difference between you and the bakery up the street. Some bakers provide a cupcake or two of their most popular cakes. Others provide a slice of what they have on hand.

A cake tasting is usually the first step toward making sure the finished cake is exactly what the bride wants. The bride will sample one to three different cake flavors that you offer; and you will work together to figure out the costs for her cake. When serving cake, serve hot coffee or tea and water.

One way you can set yourself apart from other bakeries is to discuss openly and honestly her budget. If you are genuinely concerned about accommodating her budget, your sincerity will come through. Being up-front with your clients regarding pricing is the best way to avoid misunderstandings later. Most brides will want view photographs of your recent work to weigh in on quality and workmanship of the finished products, ask for references from past brides utilizing your services and have a product tasting.

During your cake consultation, there are several key areas that should be discussed:

Design style—have her bring photos/magazine clippings of design elements she likes
Size—this is usually based on estimated number of guests
Types of frostings- buttercream, fondant, royal icing
Cake flavors and fillings
Accents—fresh flowers, gumpaste flowers, edible beading
Cake topper styles—traditional, fresh floral, sugared fruit

Pricing and delivery fees.
There are also certain questions that you should be prepared to answer regarding the baking procedures:
* Are cakes baked fresh or baked in advance and frozen?
* Are the cake layers and icings made from scratch? If so, what are the ingredients?
This may be an uncomfortable question if you use a mix, but I think it is a fair question that you should answer honestly.

CAKE CONSULTATIONS

- How many cakes do you design per weekend?
- Do you have current Department of Health or Agriculture certification?

You will want to display some of your designs on dummy cakes. Others can be seen in photographs. The dummy cakes simply show a selection of your most popular designs and the quality of your techniques.

If a custom cake is to be served, I suggest a 6" round two-layer cake, simply decorated. You may choose to charge a modest fee to cover costs. Serve the cake and beverages as soon as everyone is seated. Since this is not a social visit, waste no time asking for their thoughts on the cake they are tasting.

Be prepared for compliments as well as criticism. Everyone has an opinion and if you have difficulty hearing someone expressing a critique of your cake (the most common is: "The icing is too sweet") then tastings under these conditions, may not be a good idea for you. However, keep in mind that this is not personal. You have an opportunity to educate them.

This is the beginning point of recording their specific ideas for their cake on the contract. Conduct the consultation assuming that the order will be closed and deposit received at this meeting. Begin filling in the blanks on the agreement (available on our website) and discuss the cost of everything as you go along. Remember to be especially tactful and sensitive when discussing your cancellation policy. Make sure you mention it, but don't dwell on it.

A very important part of your agreement is the list of telephone numbers of various people that you may need to contact before the wedding and possibly on the day of the wedding. If all of those names and numbers are not yet known, be sure to follow up later. The discussion of the cake size and artistic design of the cake can be very quick and easy if a bride comes with pictures and firm ideas. However, this can become a long, drawn-out discussion if you are not prepared to step in as the professional and help the bride reach a decision.

You should not open your design idea books unless and until it becomes necessary. And do not have all of your design idea books on the table. Once you have an inkling of the cake design likes and dislikes of the bride, narrow the search and the discussion. When design discussions begin, refer to the decorated dummy cakes and hope the bride likes one of the designs displayed. Obviously, the dummies and the cakes in the portfolio will be easy and comfortable for you to do because you've done them before. If you need to look further, go to your portfolio.

If the bride finds a design that she loves, encourage her to finalize her decision because continuing to pour through a library of design idea books can become very time consuming and even confusing. Once the design decision is made, be very careful to put every minute detail on the agreement, using separate pages if necessary. Include your sketches, magazine clippings, photographs, and any color samples brought by the bride. It is very important to note the size and shape of each tier requested, as well as all design details. Write down these details.

If the couple desires a groom's cake, the same attention to detail is necessary as you complete the section of the agreement for this second cake.

At this point some calculations will be necessary. Ideally, you can quote a price without hesitation. However, if you have been asked to do something unusual or exotic, don't feel rushed to provide a quote. You may need to do some pricing research. You can always contact the bride with the exact quote the next day. You should continue to fill out the agreement completely, even without the price. That way if she is agreeable to the price, you can get a deposit and send it over to her immediately. Scanning and sending via email is the easiest way to go, as most people don't have fax machines in their home.

If she has selected a cake for which you are confident about the price, then agreement should be completely filled in. Ask the bride if she would like to go ahead and reserve her wedding date on your calendar today by signing the agreement and paying a deposit. As your business grows you will be able to mention, "dates are filling up fast." This isn't a "hard sell" per se, just the truth. When the agreement has been signed, make a copy for the bride. If you do not have a copier (or fax or printer that makes copies, assure the bride that you will mail her a copy of the contract within a few days. Often contacts can be completed in Microsoft Word and can therefore be emailed.

Occasionally, a bride will have already set up a consultation with another cake decorator and will prefer to wait before signing the agreement. This is all part of being in a service business – particularly the wedding service business. Brides will want to check out at least one other shop before making a firm decision. (Don't take it personally. It's not about you or your cakes.) It often depends on how prepared the bride is. If they are organized and have plenty of time to shop for services, they'll shop around. If time is of the essence, they may be ready to sign the contract and leave a deposit.

Whether or not the bride leaves you with a signed agreement and check (or credit card deposit), remind her that you are available if she has any questions and, again, offer your best wishes.

If the agreement has been signed, send the bride a letter thanking her for the honor of creating her wedding cake(s) and list any details that she needs to provide for you-such as a final decision on her cake board design or her cake topper. If she does not yet have a copy of the agreement, mail a copy as an enclosure with this letter.

If the bride left the consultation without having made her final decision, send a note immediately thanking her for her time in coming to discuss her wedding cake. If she left with any unanswered questions, provide the information she needed. Remind her that you are available by telephone and e-mail to answer any questions she may have and wish her well as she plans her special day.

Make it your mission to become "known" as the cake decorator whose cakes are both gorgeous and delicious and that you are a provider of EXCELLENT customer service.

16

EFFICIENCY

As you gain experience in cake decorating, you will develop your own strategies to work faster and more efficiently-thereby increasing your profit.

The following tips are offered to assist you in reaching a level of time management in your cake decorating business that others obtain only through trial and error-and lots of time.

Don't Procrastinate
As soon as an order is taken, begin a list of the steps you can do ahead of time. The goal is to keep your actual decorating time to a minimum during the final days and hours before delivery or pick-up.

Royal Icing
When planning a cake design, always consider which elements of design can be created ahead of time. Since royal icing hardens when dry, decorations can be made in advance of the cake and stored for weeks in an airtight container. Flowers, ribbon, bows, lettering, and color-flow work can be prepared weeks in advance, allowed to dry, and simply placed on the iced cake before delivery.

Gumpaste
Gumpaste decorations can also be made weeks in advance and temporarily stored in airtight containers or kept there indefinitely away from heat or moisture. Always offer gumpaste as an option to your clients as items such as flowers can look very realistic. Gumpaste is a profitable medium in which to work and classes can help you streamline your efforts for increased profitability.

Boxes and Boards
Once the cake design is planned and all possible decorations have been made in advance, still more work can be completed before the final days. If you have plenty of room, assemble the cake box and affix at least three of your business cards to the top.

The cake board can also be prepared in advance. If plywood needs to be cut to size, go the hardware store and have it cut. When using cardboard or foam core board, cut the board yourself with a craft knife. Cover the board with fabric, wrapping paper, or other material. Complete the board with a covering of cellophane and ribbon glued around the edges.
[http://www.sugarcraft.com/catalog/paper/cardboards.htm]

Refrigerating and Freezing
Several days before baking and decorating, mix buttercream icing and refrigerate. The day before decorating, divide icing into smaller bowls and color with paste food coloring. Store, tightly covered, in fridge. Bring to room temperature on decorating day.

Whenever possible avoid baking ahead of time and freezing. However, just about everybody freezes their cakes when their business picks up! When volume of business increases and wedding cake orders start coming in, freezing can become unavoidable in many cases. The cake must be protected from freezer condensation by using a moisture-proof wrapping. Suggested wrappings include:

EFFICIENCY

- greaseproof paper thoroughly covering the cake and taped
- aluminum foil, or aluminum foil and plastic wrap/greaseproof paper underneath it
- plastic self-sealing bag

When freezing cake layers, cool completely and wrap tightly in plastic wrap. Do not freeze iced cakes. When thawing, remove from freezer and set on a flat surface (kitchen counter or tabletop). Do not remove any of the wrapping until completely thawed. Be careful. You don't want to lose the cakes you now urgently need!

17

CAKE BASICS

Wedding cakes are assembled using one of four techniques: tiered, stacked, combination, or stepped. Today's cake trends are veering back towards the traditional with stacked layer cakes so we will focus on this technique.

Stacked cakes are set one on top of the other, each tier supported by an internal, unseen structure, usually wooden dowels, plastic straws, or plastic columns, cut to the exact height of the tier.

Stacked Cakes (also commonly referred to as tiered)
If you nervous about constructing stacked cakes take the time to master the simple steps to assembling them NOW. Stacked cakes are very popular and profitable so you don't want to be left out of this potential market and all of the artistic possibilities of making them.

Bridal cakes are the most familiar of stacked cakes, but cakes for other occasions can be tiered as well. When you become comfortable with stacked cakes, you can suggest them more often to your clients. Stacked and tiered cakes are often more interesting in design, and their height makes them work better as a "centerpiece" for the party.

Tiers can be round, oval, square, rectangle, triangle--any shape. They can also be a combination of shapes. Proportion is the most important consideration when planning a tiered or stacked design. Below are just a few of the limitless combinations that may be used to create a traditionally well-proportioned stacked wedding cake design:

Round or Square Tiers:
12" – 9" – 6"
14" - 10" - 6" ;
14"- 10"- 7" - 5" ;
18"-14" - 10" - 6" ;
18" - 14" - 10" - 7" ;
22" - 18" - 14" - 10" - 6";
22" - 18" - 14" - 10" - 7" - 5"

To Prepare Cake for Assembly

[http://youtube.com/watch?v=3qu9ZtV51RM]

Place base tier on a sturdy base plate of 3 or more thicknesses of corrugated cardboard. For heavy cakes, use masonite or plywood. Base can be covered with Fanci-Foil Wrap and trimmed with Tuk-N-Ruffle or use Wilton Ruffle Boards®. All from [www.wilton.com] Each tier of your cake must be on a corrugated round cut to fit. Smear a few strokes of icing on the boards to secure the cake. Fill and ice layers before assembly.

To Dowel Rod Cakes for Stacked Construction

Center a cake circle or plate one size smaller than the next tier on base tier and press it gently into icing to imprint an outline. Remove circle. Measure one dowel rod at the cake's lowest point within this circle. Using this dowel rod for measure, cut dowel rods (to fit this tier) the same size using pruning shears. If the next tier is 10-inch or less, push seven 1/4-inch dowel rods into cake down to base within circle guide. Generally the larger and more numerous the upper tiers, the more dowels needed. Very large cakes need 1/2-inch dowels in base tier.

Center a corrugated cake circle, same size as the tier to be added, on top of the base tier. Position the following tier. Repeat procedure for each additional tier. To keep stacked tiers stable, sharpen one end of a dowel rod and push through all tiers and cardboard circles to base of bottom tier. To decorate, start at top and work down.

Hints for Tiered Cakes
- Before placing separator plate or cake circle atop another tier, sprinkle a little confectioners' sugar or coconut flakes to prevent plate or circle from sticking. Letting icing crust a bit before positioning plate on cake will also prevent sticking.
- You will have fewer crumbs when icing if cakes are baked a day in advance.
- When filling or torting large layers, use less than you usually would. Your dam of icing should also be far enough from edge so filling doesn't form a bubble.
- The cake icer tip (www.wilton.com) is an invaluable timesaver in icing wedding tiers.

Budget-Conscious Tip
Budget-conscious clients who want an elaborately decorated cake may want to consider a relatively small tiered cake displayed in the reception room with simply decorated sheet cakes served from behind the scenes. (This approach is very controversial in the cake decorating community as many decorators do not offer such a service and do not believe it provides a cost savings. You can decide for yourself, based on the market you serve.)

The bride and groom slice the tiered cake and serve each other, as tradition dictates. The caterer or bride's friends are behind the scenes placing plates of sliced sheet cakes on large trays to be taken out to the reception area. The sheet cakes may be iced very simply with just a small touch of decoration or no decoration at all except for icing borders.

When quoting cake prices for this option, be consistent with your "normal" sheet cake pricing. If the tiered cake is of a very simple design and already priced economically, sheet cakes may not offer much savings.

Be fair to your-self and consistent in your pricing. Don't undercut your own prices just to get the order.

Cutting
Often a bride chooses to honor a close friend or relative by inviting her to slice and serve the bridal cake. Why is this a CRITICAL issue to your business? Simple. If the cake is cut wrong (slices too BIG) you may be blamed for not providing enough cake. This is a classic problem that happens quite frequently. If you don't provide strict cake cutting instructions, you will find an angry bride (father, mother of the bride, etc.) calling you to complain about not fulfilling the order properly. This can lead to bad word of mouth, unpaid bills, and hurt feelings.

Every wedding cake that you create should be delivered with slicing instructions. Create an instruction

CAKE BASICS

sheet on your computer, print it out and include it with every delivery. Slices should be as uniform in size as possible; usually 1" x 2" x 4".

Four inches represents the height of the two-layer tier. The slicing can be done in straight lines or in circles.

Circle-Slicing
1. Slice a circle all the way around the cake, two inches inside the outer edge.
2. Then slice one-inch servings from that outer ring. When that ring of servings is gone, again slice a two-inch circle inside the outer edge, and then slice one-inch servings from that ring.

If you slice a circle 4" deep from the edge of the cake, the slices should be 1/2" wide, or the bride may not get enough servings from their cake. The industry standard is 2"x1"x the height of the cake slices. By slicing 4" x 1" servings, you are giving each guest two servings of cake. Repeat the same slicing procedure until about a four-inch round of cake is left in the center. Slice 4 pie-shaped servings.

Straight-Line Slicing
Another method of slicing, especially for a novice, is to simply cut the cake into 2" "strips" and cut 1" slices from within these strips. The first and last slice of each strip will need to be adjusted, since they will be odd-shaped, but the cake gets less mangled in the process, and it is easier to do.

Slice a straight line straight across the back of the cake to form a wedge two-inches wide at its widest point. Slice one-inch servings across the wedge. The outermost servings will be approximately two-inch. Again, slice a straight line two-inches from the previous cross cut, and then slice one-inch servings. Straight-line slicing is often easier for someone who has never had the responsibility of slicing a wedding cake. Be sure to supply the server with clean, white, damp cloths for use in keeping the knife clean. A helper should remove and replenish cloths as necessary. Unless the wedding guests total fewer than fifty, you should suggest that at least two people be assigned to serve the bridal cake. If a groom's cake is to be served, have two people to serve it as well. You can supplement your profit by providing a cutting/serving assistant at the reception. If your schedule permits, you or someone you hire can provide this service.

NOTES:

18

DELIVERY

With gas prices skyrocketing, delivery charges have become a requirement for all businesses. This used to be a complimentary service many decorators provided. Don't be surprised if the mother of the bride is taken aback by such a fee. Calmly explain to her that this is the norm, unless she would prefer to pick up the cake. A typical charge is about $45.00 for the first 5-10 miles and an additional charge 25 – 50 cents for each additional mile. We often use the IRS mileage values (presently 50.5 cents per mile) to set the price. You cannot deduct mileage on your taxes for which you charge the customer. Another variable to consider is the difficulty of reaching the location. Mountain resorts for example or rural locations, require a premium delivery fee. This is all part of the education process and should be indicated on your website and contracts.

Another way to set delivery charges is to create delivery zones. Use Google Maps [maps.google.com]. Divide that map into various delivery zones. If all things were equal, you could simply draw circles around your location on the map to determine various pricing zones. Consider traffic patterns and real drive time when dividing your map. Charge more for greater distances, greater potential traffic and more challenging destinations. If you are near a large metropolitan area, you may charge a premium to deliver in the downtown area at 5:30 on a Friday afternoon. When calculating delivery fees, you may charge extra for parking fees, and tolls. You don't want to price yourself out of a job but you should be compensated fairly.

Prior to the day of the reception, determine what time you must leave your home to arrive at reception site on time or, preferably, a few minutes early. Allow plenty of time to drive to the reception site. Drive slower than normal, and take corners slowly and carefully. You may want to consider ordering a "Cake in Delivery" magnetic car sign so other drivers know why you're moving at a snail's pace. Vehicle Magnetic Signs Turn your car into a business vehicle and can be ordered for about $40.00 from iprint [iprint.com]

You may consider investing is a mobile GPS system if you live in a large urban area or are unfamiliar with the communities in which you will be delivering your cakes. A GPS has become an "affordable luxury" that can help you find your destination with audible, step-by-step driving directions. Granted, this is a "nice-to-have" for a new business, but if you are going to be making many deliveries, it may be something to keep in mind.

Several days before delivery, check your delivery vehicle. If your car needs cleaning, (inside and out) –do it! Don't forget to remove everything inside that could fly into and damage your cake. Vacuum the interior. If you will be transporting tiers in the trunk, clean it thoroughly and remove all loose items. Clean and inspect your car and/or drive through a car wash.

If you can drive a minivan, you will love the abundant space it provides as a cake delivery vehicle. The latest models that offer stow-and-go seats are perfect for this kind of business! Other vehicles can be a little more challenging when delivering large wedding cakes or tiers. It's better to have cakes in a large, dark, flat trunk than in the cab of a car with many windows. However, tiers can be transported in trunks, on car floors, and on seats. Measure all of these areas in your vehicle and do the math to determine where and how each tier will be loaded. If some boxes will be placed on seats and seats are not level, try placing folded towels on the seat to make the surface more level. Use a nonskid rubber mat or egg-crate foam pad to protect cakes. In lieu of rubber mats, use slightly damp (not wet) cloths under cake boxes to avoid sliding. (The best way to avoid sliding, however, is simply to drive very slowly-especially around curves and corners!)

Use bakers boxes whenever possible. For assembled cakes label each section clearly so you are not searching during assembly and use a checklist to make sure you have the entire cake. If some tiers are too large or stacked too high, use clean cardboard boxes. Whenever possible, wait until you arrive at the reception site to stack your tiers.

Turn on air conditioning in your vehicle before loading the cake(s) and load everything else before finally loading the cake.
These simple steps will help prevent icing from melting. Fondant has the tendency to weep if exposed to quickly changing hot and cool environments so try to move from cool space to cool space quickly. If possible, keep the cake away from or cover the windows, and use insulated boxes if available. A large insulated box or cover can be made by duct-taping or gluing together sheets of foil-backed insulation foam from the hardware store.

Be sure stacked cakes have a long, sharpened dowel through the center of tiers. This is not a step to skip.

Arriving at Reception Site

Wilton offers some great advice on transporting and delivering your cake.
See [http://www.wilton.com/cake/cakeprep/transporting.cfm]

Prior to arrival, you should have contacted person at the hotel or hall to confirm your delivery and verify that the table will be ready. Ask the contact person if there is a loading dock or service elevator, or ask for the best entrance to use. Are there several different banquet rooms at this location? If so, which room will YOU be delivering to? Will the air conditioning be on?

It is important to arrive at the delivery site looking neat and professional. There is no need to "dress up" - keep it casual but neat. Often the site manager, caterer, florist, and possibly members of the wedding party will be on hand when you arrive. Each of these people is a potential reference or future customer. Remember, once you've made a good impression on the site manager she will be more likely to refer business to you. Make sure that you present yourself as professionally as possible. Remember to remain calm professional, and courteous to everyone you see. The first rule to remember when arriving at the reception site is to always leave your car locked when you step away from it. On hot days, leave the car air conditioning on while taking each tier inside. Of course, always keep an extra set of keys in your pocket.

Upon entering the building, find the person in charge of this event and introduce yourself and offer your business card. This person's name should appear on the signed agreement. They should be expecting you as you just called them to confirm everything was ready, right?

Scout out the site before you carry anything in. Ask the "person in charge" to show you the cake table and confirm that the table is in the proper place and will not be moved. Check the table for level & stability. Also ask if the drapes or coverings on the tables are all in place.

Ask for the location of the exterior entry door closest to the cake table and make sure this door is unlocked. If you have previously requested the loan of a rolling cart, ask the manager about the cart at this time. Having your own collapsible delivery cart can come in handy, especially when you have a very heavy cake or a long way to walk. Consider investing in one.

Secure your vehicle at the curb next to the closest entry door. Open the door and make sure the path from this door to the cake table is clear of any obstructions. Bring in your delivery kit and place on the floor beside the cake table. Do not place any of your things on any tables other than the cake table.

Next, bring in the cake. If you car is blocking a delivery area, move it as soon as the cake is inside.

After the cake is completely set up, carefully remove everything from the cake table and clean up everything in the area where you worked. Look carefully at the cake table from all angles to ensure that the cake is perfectly level and centered. Take this opportunity to photograph the cake.

Ask the event manager to come to the cake table and look at the cake. Ask her to sign the bottom of the agreement where it states that the cake was set up as stated in the agreement. Give her the slicing instruction sheet and the box for the top tier-the anniversary tier (if applicable). Although it is stated on the slicing instruction sheet, be sure that she understands which items are to be returned to you and point out to her any decorative items on that cake that are not edible.

Some bakeries charge a flat equipment deposit. You may want to charge the replacement value (ask for a separate check or keep the credit card on file) & tell the bride that you will return the check when/if the items are returned. This should all be documented on the cake agreement/contract. You will want to set a time frame, and specify that they should be clean. If they are returned with missing pieces, or very late, you can tell the bride that you will cash the check, remove any charges, and return the difference to her. You can put your name & phone # on your plates, to assure their return. Leave a bag or box at the reception, along with a list of items to be returned to you.

Your photos of the cake immediately after set-up also serve as "proof" as to the condition of the cake when delivered. While it is rare, there are occasions when a cake decorator has had the unfortunate experience of damage done to their cakes due to circumstances beyond their control. After you leave, the caterers may try to move the table or bump into the table by accident. Children may arrive in the reception site before the wedding party and stick their fingers in the cake. Your photos-taken from all angles-show that you set up the cake properly, in the agreed-upon location, and that the cake was in perfect condition when you left.

19

ORGANIZATION

Lists are the key to organizing your work and managing your time.

As has been indicated through out this book, taking the time to write down everything about your business frees the mind to be creative. This includes everything that must be done to fulfill each contract.

Keep a notebook of contracts pending. This notebook will contain:
- The original and a copy of the signed agreement
- Any sketches, color samples, magazine clippings, and other design inspiration pieces
- "Important Information" list:
  - Names of everyone connected with the order: bride, groom, mother of the bride, wedding planner. Be sure to make a particular note of the person who is responsible for payment.
  - Addresses and phone numbers. Include exact address of reception site and bride's new address after the wedding (if her address will change).
  - Directions to reception site and more importantly specific instructions on the reception location once you arrive.
  - Wedding Day Cell Phone Numbers (for emergency use only!). This list should include cell phone and all other phone numbers for the bride (you should never have to use this number on the wedding day, however!) mother of the bride, maid of honor, person at reception site in charge of this event, florist, photographer, and caterer.

CHECKLIST for SUCCESS
- "One Month Before Wedding Date" checklist
- "One Week Before Wedding Date" to do list
- "Day Before Delivery" to do list
- "Delivery Day" to do list
- "Follow-Up" list
- "Serving Instruction Sheet"
- Advance-purchase ingredient and supply buying list
- Last-week ingredient and supply buying list

The detailed nature of the sample lists below ensures that nothing is forgotten, that you can handle any emergency and that you are a professional every step of the way. Customize this list to suit your own needs.

One Month Before Wedding Date
Purchase non-perishable items, such as:
- Decorator tips
- Base cake board (plywood, Masonite or foam core)
- Cardboard rounds (include rounds that will be used simply to handle/move large tiers)
- Fabric and ribbon for base cake board
- Cake topper
- Pillars and separator plates
- Baker's box for top tier

START A CAKE BUSINESS TODAY

Clean boxes for transporting tiers to reception site
Take inventory of other items that are normally on hand, but which may be running low:
- Pastry bags
- Cellophane (to cover fabric on base cake board)_Packing tape (to tape fabric and cellophane to bottom of cake board)
- White glue (to affix ribbon to edge of covered cake board)
- Paste food colors
- Gumpaste, fondant
- Confectioner's sugar
- Plastic wrap (wrap cake layers until ready to ice)
- Dowel rods

Write list of all grocery items to be purchased during week before delivery
Prepare base cake board
Assemble anniversary cake box (the box the couple will use to take home the top tier)
Make as many cake decorations as possible (i.e., gumpaste or royal icing flowers and decorations, etc.)
Check records to make sure balance of payment has been received
Prepare "delivery kit" - items that may come in handy at delivery.

A delivery kit contains:

- Map to reception/party site
- Telephone # of site
- Telephone # of contact person
- Contract / invoice / delivery form
- Bride's top ornament
- Cutting knife & server set (in case one is not provided)
- Angled spatula
- Piping bag(s) filled with icing (one bag with each color; secure end with twist-tie and wrap in plastic wrap)
- Container of icing
- One of each decorating tips used on cake (for touch-ups, if necessary)
- Decorating bags
- Tips used to decorate the cake
- Couplers
- Spatulas
- Flowers : Fresh or silk flowers/greenery
- Flower spikes
- Picture of the cake
- Columns/pillars, plus extras (in case of necessary last-minute design changes)
- Pillar pruning shears
- Any decorations or cake topper that will be added on site
- Ribbon
- Tulle
- Tablecloths if necessary to cover ugly tables
- Florist's Wire
- Scissors that can also cut wire
- Toothpicks
- Meat or kabob skewers
- Paper towels

ORGANIZATION

- Wax or parchment paper
- Wet washcloth in plastic bag or moist wipes
- Dry cloth
- A level
- Shims to correct uneven tables
- Measuring tape
- Camera, film/extra memory card, and extra battery
- Business cards and a holder
- A congratulations card for the Couple
- An ink pen
- Clear tape & double-sided tape
- Small hot-glue gun
- Dressmakers pins (for securing fabric when necessary)
- Band-aids
- Apron
- Garbage bag
- Latex gloves
- Doorstop
- Extension cords
- Duct tape
- Distilled water
- Color for water
- Flower Holder Ring

For the Bride-
- Cutting/serving instructions specific to this cake
- Latex gloves for the server(s)
- Box for Anniversary cake
- List of pieces to be returned
- Box or bag for plates & columns

One Week Before Wedding Date
Monday (for Saturday delivery):

- Contact florist if agreement states that she will supply and/or arrange flowers on the cake. Confirm her arrival time at reception site and the time you will have the cake set up and ready for her flowers.
- Contact photographer to request photographs of the cake for your portfolio.
- Contact site manager. Confirm your arrival time and ask if the facility has a rolling cart that you may use to bring in the cake.
- Purchase all cake and icing ingredients.

Tuesday:
- Make buttercream icing and refrigerate.
- Double check all pre-made decorations (extras should have been made in case of breakage)
- Pull all necessary pans, cooling racks, and cardboard rounds.
- Clean car or van interior. Wash sheets that will be used to cover van seat or floor surfaces.
- Fill delivery vehicle with gasoline.

Wednesday:
Marketing, blogging, tastings, etc.

Thursday:
Bake, cool, trim, and wrap all cake layers.

Friday:
- Remove buttercream from refrigerator and allow to come to room temperature.
- Ice and decorate cake.
- Check delivery kit. Add icing and appropriate tips to kit.
- Photograph cake if decorating is complete today.
- Prepare car or van for loading tomorrow. Place magnetic business sign on vehicle.

Delivery Day

- Complete any unfinished decorating.
- Photograph cake.
- Load delivery vehicle:
- Delivery kit (see contents list above)
- Cake
- Directions to reception site

Follow-Up
- Mail thank you notes to bride and groom and, if applicable, to other party involved in order or payment.
- If cake board, separate plates, and columns (etc.) are not returned by the deadline, call bride's mother (or responsible party) to remind them that you will cash the equipment check or charge their card unless items are returned by certain date.
- Upload cake image to your website and blog.

NOTES:

CONCLUSION

Starting any new business can be very exciting and a little frightening! When you have determined that a cake decorating business is the business in which you are going to invest your time, your money, and your energy---do everything within your power to make it happen. Read everything you can find on baking, recipes, and starting a business. Talk to other bakers, wedding service providers, and owners of home-based businesses of any type. Join the forums on Cakecentral, start blogging, and reach out in every way to your community of peers.

Set goals for your business. Constantly review your goals to make sure you remain on course. When you find that something is not working for your business, either figure out a way to make it work or re-evaluate your goals in that area.

NOTES:

CLASSIC RECIPES

Cakes

BASIC WHITE CAKE
2 cups all-purpose flour
1 tablespoon baking powder
1 teaspoon salt
3/4 cup shortening
1 1/2 cups sugar
1 1/2 teaspoons vanilla
1 cup milk
5 egg whites

Grease and lightly flour two 9-inch round cake pans. Combine flour, baking powder and salt. In a mixer bowl, beat shortening using medium speed for about 30 seconds. Add sugar and vanilla and beat until fluffy. Add dry ingredients and milk alternately to beaten mixture, beating on low speed after each addition. Wash beaters. In a small mixer bowl, beat egg whites until stiff peaks form. Gently fold into batter. Turn into pans. Bake at 375 about 20 minutes or until cake tests done. Cool 10 minutes in pans. Remove from pans and cool on wire racks.

FUDGE CAKE
12 ounces semi-sweet chocolate, coarsely chopped
5 teaspoons espresso or strong coffee
2 cups
2 cups sugar
1 cup butter
6 eggs, separated, room temperature
1 cup all-purpose flour
Confectioners sugar for garnish, optional

Position the rack in center of oven and preheat to 350. Lightly butter a 9-inch springform pan. Dust pan with flour and tap out excess. In top of double boiler over hot, not simmering water, melt together espresso and chocolate, stirring occasionally. Remove the pan from heat and cool until tepid. In large bowl, using hand-held electric mixer set at medium high speed, cream sugar and butter together until light and fluffy. One at a time, add egg yolks to mixture, beating well after each addition. Beat in flour. In large grease-free bowl, using hand-held mixer at medium high speed, beat egg whites until they form stiff, shiny peaks.

Fold 1/4 of the whites into chocolate mixture to lighten. Then fold in remaining whites. Fold in butter and flour
mixture. Scrape batter into prepared pan and bake 60-70 minutes or until top is crusty and cracked and the middle is until slightly moist. Remove cake to wire rack to cool completely. Remove sides of springform pan and transfer cake to serving plate.

CLASSIC RECIPES

POPPYSEED CAKE
1 1/2 cups all-purpose flour
1 1/2 cups whole-wheat flour
1/3 cup poppyseeds
2 1/2 teaspoons baking soda
1/2 teaspoons salt
3/4 cup butter or margarine
1 1/2 cups honey
1 teaspoons vanilla
4 eggs
1/2 cup buttermilk or sour milk
1 small banana, mashed
1/2 cup raisins

Grease and lightly flour a 10-inch tube pan. Combine flours, poppyseeds, baking soda, and salt. Beat butter about 30 seconds at medium speed. Add honey and vanilla; beat until fluffy. Add eggs, one at a time, beating 1 minute after each. Combine buttermilk or sour milk and banana. Add dry ingredients and buttermilk mixture alternately to egg mixture, beating after each addition. Stir in raisins. Turn into pan and spread evenly.

Bake at 350 for 50 to 55 minutes or until cake tests done. Cool 15 minutes in pan. Invert onto a wire rack and remove pan. Cool thoroughly.

PUMPKIN SPICE CAKE WITH ORANGE SAUCE
1/2 cup margarine
3/4 cup sugar
2 large eggs
3/4 cup mashed cooked pumpkin
1 teaspoon vanilla extract
1 1/2 cups all-purpose flour
1 1/2 teaspoons baking powder
1/4 teaspoon salt
1 1/2 teaspoons pumpkin pie spice
Powdered sugar
Orange Sauce (see recipe below)

Beat margarine at medium speed with electric mixer until creamy; gradually add sugar, beating well. Add eggs, 1 at a time, beating until blended after each addition. Stir in pumpkin and vanilla. Combine flour plus next 3 ingredients; gradually add to sugar mixture, beating at low speed until blended after each addition. Pour into greased floured 9-inch round cake pan. Bake at 350 for 20 minutes or until wooden pick inserted in center comes out clean. Cool in pan on wire rack 10 minutes; remove from pan, cool on wire rack. Place a paper doily over cake; sift powdered sugar through wire-mesh strainer over doily. Remove the doily and serve with Orange Sauce.

Orange Sauce
1/3 cup light brown sugar
1 tablespoon cornstarch
1 1/2 cups orange juice
1 teaspoon lemon juice

Whisk together all ingredients in heavy saucepan until blended. Bring mixture to boil over medium-heat, whisking constantly; boil, whisking constantly, 1 minute. Serve warm or cool. Makes 1 3/4 cups.

LEMON CHIFFON CAKE
2 cups cake flour, sifted
1 cup sugar
1/2 cup sugar
1 teaspoon baking powder
1 teaspoon baking soda
1/4 teaspoon Salt
1/2 cup sunflower oil
1 teaspoon grated lemon zest (about 2 lemons)
1/4 cup fresh lemon juice, (1 to 2 lemons)
1 tablespoon pure vanilla extract
1 teaspoon lemon extract
7 large egg whites

Preheat oven to 325. Prepare 12 cup (about 9) bundt pan with non-stick coating. In large mixing bowl, sift together flour, 1 cup sugar, baking powder, and baking soda, salt. In small cup or bowl, mix oil, lemon zest, lemon juice, vanilla extract, and lemon extract. In large stainless steel bowl, beat egg whites until white and foamy. Slowly add remaining 1/2 cup sugar plus beat just until stiff peak form. Do not over beat. Make a well in center of flour mixture.

Place wet ingredients into well. Add 1/4 whites into well; mix gently until all ingredients are blended. Gently fold in remaining whites using rubber spatula. Pour batter into prepared pan. Bang pan on counter to remove any air bubbles. Bake about 30 minutes until golden plus top feels springy or until cake tester inserted into center comes out clean. Cool on wire rack 1/2 hour. Loosen sides with small knife if necessary. Remove cake from pan; cool 1/2 hour. Store in airtight container or serve immediately.

Lemon Vanilla Glaze: mix 1 cup confectioners sugar with 1 teaspoon vanilla extract, 1/4 teaspoon lemon extract. Add water if necessary; mix until smooth.
Drizzle glaze over cake. Lightly dust confectioner's sugar over.

CHOCOLATE ANGEL FOOD CAKE
12 large egg whites
3/4 cup cake flour
1 teaspoon vanilla extract
1 teaspoon cream of tartar
1-1/4 cups sugar
1/4 teaspoon salt
1/4 cup cocoa powder
1/4 cup chocolate syrup

Preheat oven to 325F. Beat egg whites in a large bowl for a few minutes before adding the cream of tartar. Beat until egg whites stand in stiff peaks. Combine the sugar and salt (if using granulated sugar instead of superfine bar sugar, sift it twice). Slowly add the sugar to the beaten egg whites and also add the vanilla. Continue beating until peaks are not only stiff but shiny. Sift the flour and the cocoa powder together and fold into the mixture (try to deflate the egg whites as little as possible). Spoon into an ungreased angel food cake tin. While doing this, be sure there are no air bubbles and push the mixture into the sides around the tin. When about 1/3 full, drizzle the chocolate sauce over the surface. Using a spoon or spatula, plunge about 3 times into the batter for a marbled effect. Add 1/3 more batter and repeat step, plunging in different areas than last time. Now add the remainder of the batter. Keep in mind that the syrup will settle to the bottom of the tin during baking if you use too much or it is all in one area. Put in oven on a middle or lower rack (so it doesn't brown too quickly) and bake for 50-60 minutes. Remove from the oven and turn upside down and using the small feet on the rim of the tin. Place on the counter to cool. It is important to have the cake upside down other wise it will be heavy.

If your tin does not have feet use a narrow neck bottle to fit through the hole of the center of the pan. Let it stay until completely cooled. Run a serrated knife around the inside and outside of the tin to loosen. Also do the same around the bottom of the tin once it has been removed from the sides. Serve slices using a serrated knife in a sawing motion. Serves 12-16.

OLD FASHIONED CHOCOLATE FUDGE CAKE
2 cups flour
2 cups sugar
1-1/2 teaspoons baking soda
1/4 teaspoon salt
1/2 cup cocoa
1/2 cup oil
1 cup buttermilk
2 eggs, beaten
3 teaspoons vanilla
3/4 cup hot water
4 tablespoons cocoa
6 tablespoons milk
1 stick butter
1 box (1 pound) powdered sugar
1 tablespoon vanilla
1 cup chopped pecans

Sift together the flour, sugar, soda, salt, and cocoa. Add oil, buttermilk, eggs, vanilla and hot water; mix well. Bake in greased 9 x 13 inch pan at 350 for 30-40 minutes. For icing make a paste of the cocoa and milk in a saucepan. Add butter and bring to a boil, stirring constantly. Remove from heat and add powdered sugar and vanilla. Beat and then add pecans. Pour over still hot cake in baking pan.

BUTTERMILK POUND CAKE
1/2 cup butter or margarine
1/2 cup shortening
2 cups sugar
5 eggs
2 1/2 teaspoons vanilla
3 cups all-purpose flour, sifted
1/2 teaspoon salt
1/2 teaspoon baking powder
1/2 teaspoon baking soda
1 cup buttermilk

Preheat oven to 325. Grease and flour a 10-inch tube pan. Cream butter, shortening, and sugar together in mixing bowl until light and fluffy. Add eggs one at a time, beating well after each addition. Blend in vanilla. Sift flour, salt, baking powder, and soda together, add to creamed mixture alternately with milk, beginning and ending with flour mixture. Mix well after each addition. Spoon batter into prepared pan. Bake for 1 hour and 15 minutes or until toothpick inserted one inch from edge comes out clean. Cool in pan for 10 minutes; turn out onto wire rack and cool completely.

DOUBLE LEMON CAKE
3 cups flour plus extra for dusting pans
1 tablespoon baking powder
1/2 teaspoon salt
1 cup butter plus extra for pans
2 cups sugar
4 large eggs
1 cup milk
1 teaspoon vanilla extract

Lemon Filling
1-1/2 cups sugar
6 tablespoons flour
1/4 teaspoon salt
3 large egg yolks
1/2 cup fresh lemon juice
1/3 cup grated lemon zest
1/2 cup butter
Topping
3/4 cup sugar
3 tablespoons cornstarch
1/4 teaspoon salt
1 tablespoon butter
2 tablespoons grated lemon zest
1/3 cup fresh lemon juice

For the cake, sift flour, baking powder and salt together. Grease and lightly flour three 9-in cake pans. In a large
mixing bowl, cream butter with sugar, using an electric mixer, if possible. Add eggs, one at a time, mixing well after each addition. The mixture should be smooth and creamy. Using a spoon, add 1/3 of the flour and fold into the batter with 1/3 of the milk. Repeat until flour and milk are incorporated into batter. It is important that the ingredients are folded in; the batter should not be beaten after flour has been introduced. Stir in vanilla. Distribute batter evenly among 3 cake pans and bake in a preheated 350 oven for about 30 minutes or until layers are golden brown and spring back when gently pressed in the middle. Cool for about 5 minutes and turn layers out of pans. For the filling, combine sugar, flour and salt in a heavy saucepan. Add 2 cups water and mix well. Cook over low-medium heat, stirring occasionally until thick. Add egg yolks, lemon juice, lemon zest and butter and cook for 12 minutes, stirring occasionally. Cool.

For the topping: mix sugar, cornstarch and salt in a heavy saucepan. Add 3/4 cup water gradually. Bring to a boil, stirring constantly. Boil 1 minute. Remove from heat and stir in butter and lemon rind. Gradually stir in lemon juice. Cool To assemble: cover 1st and 2nd layers w/lemon filling. Spread generously. Coat top of 3rd layer and sides of cake with clear lemon topping. Filling and topping must be thoroughly cooled before using.

Icings

BUTTER CREAM ICINGS

WHITE BUTTER CREAM ICING
ADD IN ORDER GIVEN:
1 cup Crisco (no more than 1 1/2 cups) (Crisco is solid vegetable shortening)
1 teas CLEAR Vanilla extract
1/4 teas CLEAR Almond extract
1/4 teas CLEAR Butter flavoring
1/2 cup Milk or water (as preferred)
Pinch of salt
2 lb Confectioner's sugar; sift if lumpy or using a hand mixer
1/4 cup Cream Whip Icing Base *see note next

OPTIONAL: Use this only when making buttercream flowers - to crust them harder. They are easier to handle.
Add all ingredients except sugar. Add sugar gradually. You do not have to put all the sugar in, if icing is becoming too stiff. Mix on medium speed until light and fluffy. Keep icing covered at all times. This recipe will cover one cake mix and do decorations.

NOTES: Keeps un-refrigerated for 2 weeks in reasonably cool room. Keeps indefinitely in fridge. Can use milk or water. There is no difference in taste, but purple decorations made using milk, won't fade to blue.

IF USING A HAND-HELD MIXER: Don't add all the sugar so you won't ruin the mixer. When icing is nice and fluffy, THEN add the rest of the sugar, or enough to get it to spreadable consistency. If mixer gets hot (set a timer!), turn it off for 20 minutes to cool down or its ruined!

BUTTER ICING Butter melts just setting out, so it also melts in the bag in your warm hands. In recipe above, you can substitute butter for Crisco—same amounts—or substitute half the butter for Crisco. When butter icing is requested, caution customers that the decorations won't be as precise.

PRACTICE ICING
This recipe is really greasy; but simple to use when learning or practicing making decorations.
1 cup Vegetable Shortening
3-4 tb water or milk
1/2 teaspoon Vanilla
Extract 1 lb Confectioners' Sugar
Add in order given and beat until stiff peaks form. Cover bowl. Use cold.

EASY CHOCOLATE FUDGE BUTTERCREAM ICING
Make BUTTERCREAM ICING as above, then add to any amount of icing; Dry Hershey's Cocoa < not drink mix > until the buttercream icing becomes the nice rich chocolate color and taste you prefer.
If you want a stronger chocolate taste, just add more cocoa. Additional amounts of water (or milk) will be needed to be added to thin it back down to proper consistency.

CHOCOLATE ICING 2
1/3 cup Cocoa
1 lb Confectioners' sugar

1/4 cup Margarine
1/2 cup Evaporated milk
1/2 teas Vanilla
Mix cocoa with the powder sugar. Warm remaining ingredients until margarine melts.. Slowly add cocoa mixture and beat until creamy.

SEMI-CREAM ICING
3/4 cup Crisco
3/4 cup Non-fat dry milk
2 tb Corn syrup
2 tb Flour
1 lb Confectioner's sugar
2 teas Flavoring
1/2 cup Water
Combine ingredients in mixer bowl. Depending on the sugar used, you may need to adjust the amount of water used. The flour and dry milk help take out the sweetness. Refrigerate cake.

VANILLA ICING
1/4 cup Margarine
1/4 cup Half and half
1 teas Vanilla
1 cup Brown sugar
2 cup Confectioners' sugar
Mix margarine, half and half and brown sugar and bring to a boil. Cook 5 minutes. Add confectioners' sugar and vanilla. Drizzle over cake.

CREAM CHEESE ICING
3/4 cup Margarine
12 oz Cream cheese; softened
2 teaspoons Vanilla
1 1/2 lb Confectioner's sugar; sifted
1 cup Pecan halves (garnish); opt.
Using an electric mixer, blend the first three ingredients together. Add confectioner's sugar gradually, beating
continually until smooth. If necessary, add water to thin. This icing isn't so sweet tasting, but is rather soft and offwhite in color.

WHITE CHOCOLATE ICING
3/4 cup white Merckens coating chocolate; melted
2 1/2 Tablespoons flour
1 Cup Milk
1 Cup butter or margarine, softened
1 Cup sugar
1 1/2 Teaspoon vanilla
In a medium saucepan, combine white summer coating, which has been melted. Add flour. Blend in milk, cook over medium heat, stirring constantly until mixture is very thick. Cool completely. In a large mixing bowl cream butter, sugar and vanilla. Beat until light and fluffy, about 3 minutes. Gradually add completely cooled summer coating mixture. Beat at high speed until it is the consistency of whipped cream. Refrigerate cake. NOTE: Of course, this could also be made using ANY flavor coating chocolate cake in decorative patterns.

CLASSIC RECIPES

DECORATING BUTTERCREAM FOR PROFESSIONALS
RECIPE FOR 20 QT BOWL:
3 lb Shortening (Alpine or Sweetex comes in a 50 lb cube)
1 cup flavorings
1 teas Salt
1 Crisco can of water (more or less)
30 lb Confectioners' sugar (just a guideline - add what you need to make the icing workable)

RECIPE FOR A LARGER BOWL: 50 pounds powdered (confectioners') sugar 6 pounds cold water 25 pounds emulsified cake shortening (Alpine or Sweetex comes in a 50 lb cube) 3 ounces salt 3 ounces vanilla Blend the powdered sugar, water, salt, and vanilla to a smooth paste. This will be very stiff and should be mixed at low speed, only long enough to saturate and to remove all the lumps from the sugar. Add the shortening in one-or two-pound portions and mix at medium speed until completely incorporated. Caution: scrape down the sides of the mixing bowl thoroughly in this stage: do not over mix. Over mixing the buttercream will cause excessive aeration that will be particularly detrimental to smooth figure work. The buttercream works best if it is mixed at least a day before it is to be used. After it sits it will become aerated, but most of the bubbles should disappear when it is re-mixed. Caution should be employed here: the re-mixing should be done by hand or on the lowest speed with a machine. It is best to re-mix only the amount needed for short periods of time. If, in the process of decorating, the buttercream seems too tacky or too elastic it may be due to the sugar. Only powdered cane sugar will produce the best quality buttercream for decorating.

ROLLED BUTTERCREAM ICING
1 recipe Wilton regular buttercream having
1 cup Crisco to
2 lb confectioners' sugar - or about (no meringue, milk or butter)

add:
1/4 cup glucose
Add more powdered sugar until no longer sticky. Make Wilton gum paste recipe and combine buttercream and gum paste. Doesn't dry as fast as fondant.

ROLLED BUTTERCREAM FONDANT
Make mixture of equal parts -
1 cup or 1 tb or etc. Crisco (solid)
1 cup or 1 TB or etc. Karo
Flavoring of choice
Enough confectioners' sugar to make a stiff dough
Knead until nice and smooth. It can be hand molded, molded in the candy molds, rolled out, shaped, etc.

LEMON BUTTER FROSTING
1 teaspoon Lemon rind; grated
6 tb Butter
3 cup Confectioners' sugar; sifted
1/4 cup Lemon juice; approx.
1 teaspoon Salt

Add lemon rind to butter; cream well Add part of the sugar gradually, blending after each addition. Add remaining sugar, alternately with lemon juice, until spreadable consistency. Beat thoroughly after each addition.

Add salt. Makes enough frosting to cover tops and sides of two 9-inch layers or tops and sides two 8 x 8 x 2-inch layers.

ROYAL ICINGS
Royal Icing is used for decorations on candies or delicate flowers, etc. for cakes.
ROYAL ICING WITH MERINGUE POWDER
This is your choice for an "all-around" Royal icing. Good to use for Lace pieces.
ADD IN ORDER GIVEN: BEAT WITH MIXER:
6 tb warm water
3 tb Meringue powder *
1/4 teas CLEAR Almond extract *
ADD GRADUALLY:
1 lb Confectioners' sugar
Combine warm water, meringue powder and almond extract. Beat on medium speed until the meringue powder/ water mixture resembles frothy egg whites and meringue powder is all dissolved. Add confectioners' sugar gradually, beating on low-medium speed until icing is light, fluffy and holds its shape. It should stand in peaks and have a dull appearance. This can take up to 15 minutes.

TIP: IF ADDED STRENGTH IS NEEDED, ALSO ADD: 1/2 teas Cream of tartar AND/OR 1 tb Gum Arabic
* Add optional cream of tartar and gum Arabic just before Confectioners' sugar is added.
NOTES: Utensils should be grease free. Keep icing covered at all times with a damp cloth. Crust cannot be used! To restore texture, simply re-beat. For thinner consistency of icing, add a tablespoon of water; continue beating. Air holes (from beating on too-high speed) will cause decorations to be very brittle and break easily.
High humidity can make pieces brittle also. Can store un-refrigerated for up to 2 weeks. Will keep indefinitely refrigerated. Using a hand-held mixer, wait until icing is ready before adding the last cup of confectioners' sugar.

LACE PIECES A wonderful way to use lace points with the cakes is to hang them under the cakes. Between the separations just behind the base borders. Put fresh royal on top of each lace point with tip 2 or 3 and then attach to the bottom of the separator plate after the cake is delivered and set up on the table.
If the florist is doing real flowers on your cake wait till he or she is through to hang the lace. They tend to knock it off and you have to wait till they are through and put them back. It is easier to just hang them after they get done.

LARGE RECIPE FOR ROYAL ICING
1 1/2 cup Warm water
12 tb Meringue powder * (beat; add:)
4 lb Powdered sugar
1 teas Almond extract
Beat until it loses it's shine and stands in peaks.

ROYAL ICING
Mix until foamy:
2/3 cup lukewarm water
1/4 cup deluxe meringue powder
Add on low speed the confectioners' sugar mixture consisting of
2 lb confectioners' Sugar
1 1/2 tb Gum Arabic
1/2 teas cream of tartar
This can be kept in a tightly covered glass jar for a long period of time until used up.

Glazes

BUTTERSCOTCH GLAZE
1/4 cup Butter
1 cup Confectioners' sugar
1/4 cup Brown sugar
1 teas Vanilla or rum extract
2 tb Milk

In sauce pan combine butter, brown sugar and milk. Bring to full boil. Remove from heat. Add sugar and extract. Beat until smooth. Add more milk for consistency you want to drizzle over cake top.

SUGAR GLAZE
1/2 cup Confectioners' sugar
1/4 teas Vanilla extract
2 teas Warm water

Sift the confectioners' sugar into a small bowl. Sprinkle 2 teas of warm water and the vanilla over the sugar and stir until smooth. If the glaze seems stiff, add more water, drop by drop, until it reaches drizzling consistency. To use the glaze: drizzle over cooled turnovers with a fork. Alternatively, scrape the glaze into a sturdy plastic bag; snip off a tiny portion of the corner and use the bag to pipe the glaze decoratively on turnovers. This makes enough glaze for 10 turnovers. It should be made shortly before using, since it hardens quickly on contact with air.

CHOCOLATE RUM GLAZE
4 oz Semisweet Chocolate coating *
6 tb Butter
1 tb Light corn syrup
1 tb Dark rum (optional)

In heavy saucepan on low heat, melt broken chocolate with butter, stirring constantly until smooth. Remove from heat. Stir in corn syrup and rum. Place torte upside down on a rack over tray to catch excess glaze. Spread a very thin layer of glaze over top and sides of torte to set surface. Chill 15 minutes to firm glaze. Re-heat remaining glaze to thin and pour over top and sides of torte. When glaze is firm, remove cake from rack to large plate. Using chocolate shaver, * shave chocolate to decorate top and sides, if desired. For shiny glaze, store cake at room temperature until serving time.

GANACHE 1
Ganache is an icing made up of whipping cream and chocolate chips.
2 cups Heavy Cream to 1 lb chocolate chips.

Warm the whipping cream and add the chocolate chips, stirring continually until all of the chips are melted and the icing is very glossy and smooth. Set aside to cool. Check occasionally and when the icing begins to thicken it can be poured over a cake on a cooling rack. (Put a tray underneath to catch the drippings.) If you need it for a filling or want to whip it to use like buttercream it needs to cool longer. Basic borders can be done..

GANACHE 2
3-12 oz. bags chocolate chips
1 pt half/half
1/4 cup sugar
1/4 cup butter

Mix as above

BITTERSWEET CHOCOLATE GANACHE
6 oz High quality bittersweet Chocolate
1 cup Whipping cream
1 tb Brandy
1 teas Vanilla

Chop or grate chocolate into fine crumbs. Heat cream until small bubbles form around the edge; pour cream onto chocolate. Process or stir to melt chocolate completely. The mixture will be quite liquid. Let it cool. Beat in brandy and vanilla. This frosting takes several hours at room temperature to achieve spreading consistency. To speed the process, refrigerate. Stir occasionally to assure even chilling. Use as a frosting.
NOTE: This should be made with a blender.

FRESH STRAWBERRY GLAZE
1/2 cup Strawberries; thinly sliced
3/4 cup Sugar 3/4 cup Strawberry syrup OR 3/4 cup Strawberry syrup and water
3 1/2 teas Cornstarch
1 tb Water
1/2 teas Lemon juice

Combine strawberries and sugar; let stand 30 minutes. Bring to a boil, and simmer 3 minutes. Strain through wire sieve. Measure strawberry syrup, adding water if necessary to make 3/4 cup. Pour into small saucepan. Mix cornstarch, water, and lemon juice; add to strawberry syrup. Bring to a boil, and cook gently 4 to 6 minutes, or until thickened.
Cool slightly and spread over cake which has been frosted with Fresh Strawberry Frosting, letting it run down on sides. Let stand about 1 hour to allow glaze to become firm.
NOTES:

TORTES and CAKE FILLINGS
Any GREAT cake recipes deserves a GREAT cake filling! You can spread filling in the center, between the layers, or split each layer in half and add filling as a torte.

WARNING: DO NOT use puddings or those made with MILK or CREAM, unless you plan to store the cake in the
refrigerator until eaten, as bacteria can cause a very "subtle" food poisoning that may not show up for 1-2 days, but can be very dangerous.

TO TORTE: Split each cake layer in half horizontally using a professional cake slicer or a serrated edged knife. Slide a card board circle between the two slices and lift off the top one. Place a circle of icing on top outside edge of each one, (piped from a decorator bag; open coupler only, no tip needed.) This makes a "wall" to keep filling from oozing out.

TO ASSEMBLE: Starting with bottom slice, slide the next one off the card board circle * onto the bottom layer. Proceed with other layers-slices until assembled.

NOTE: Icing should NOT be stiff for spreading or cake crumbs pull off into the icing.

PINEAPPLE FILLING (Very good with yellow cake)
2 1/2 cups Buttercream icing
1 small can Crushed pineapple; drain well 2-3 drops
Oil of Pineapple *
Mix all ingredients together. Blend well. Make "wall" of regular buttercream icing as directed above. Spread filling evenly over each layer. This filling is very thin and good!

CHOCOLATE NUT FILLING
2 cup Powdered sugar
1 oz Chocolate
Few grains salt
2 tb Melted butter
1 tb Cream
2/3 cup Chopped nuts
1 teas Vanilla
Melt chocolate over hot water. Sift sugar. Add butter and cream. Beat until smooth. Add chocolate, salt, flavoring, and nuts.

SOFT BUTTERCREAM FILLING
1 cup Granulated sugar
3 tb Meringue powder
2/3 cup Hot water
2 cup Crisco
2 lb Confectioners' sugar
1 tb Creme Bouquet *

Beat granulated sugar, meringue powder and hot water to a stiff peak. Add flavoring & Crisco. Mix on low speed. Add powdered sugar slowly, (1/2 cup at a time) while mixer is running. After all sugar is added; beat on medium speed for 5 minutes.

BAKING TIPS PART II

MEASURING INGREDIENTS:
Measure ingredients carefully, using spoons and measuring cups made especially for this purpose. All measurements are usually level. Pre-Measure: Whether you are preparing to bake a two-layer birthday cake or a five-tiered wedding cake, put all ingredients on counter before mixing cake or icing. Measure all ingredients in advance, setting aside each ingredient container after it is measured

TO SIFT OR NOT TO SIFT? All-purpose flour usually doesn't need to be sifted; simply stir it lightly with a spoon before measuring. When sifted flour is called for, the ingredients list will say "1 cup sifted flour." This means sift the flour and then measure. If it says, "1 cup flour, sifted," the flour should be measured and then sifted.

CAKE FLOUR, which has been finely milled, has a tendency to form lumps. It should always be sifted before using.

BE PREPARED:
Make sure you have all the ingredients before you start making the batter. Use the pan sizes suggested and prepare the baking pans carefully as the recipe states. If you are greasing the pans, solid vegetable shortening is best to use. If the directions call for a lined pan, cut parchment or waxed paper to fit the bottom of the pan, then grease the pan before and after placing the paper inside.

START A CAKE BUSINESS TODAY

Prepare Pans
Butter and flour all pans (or use a convenient baking pan spray) and place all pans in fridge. Remove pan from fridge a few minutes before filling pan with batter. Baking cake layers early in the morning on the day before delivery or pick-up leaves the rest of the day (and evening if necessary) for decorating.

Multiple Cakes
When baking several cakes, begin mixing batter for the second cake about 10 minutes before first cake is completely baked. When first cake is removed from oven, second cake will be ready to slide into the oven.

Large Pans
When using any large pan for the first time, make a note of exactly how many recipes of batter were required to fill the pan (i.e., 12" x 2" round pan uses 1-1/4 pound cake recipe).

DUSTING PANS
Occasionally you will find recipes that call for dusting the pans. This helps the cake develop a thin, crisp crust and prevents the cake from absorbing the fat used to grease the pan. Use about one tablespoon all-purpose flour for dusting each pan. Shake and tilt the pan until the bottom and sides have a fine coating. Don't over-do it. Hold the pan upside down and tap it gently so excess flour falls away.

PREHEATING OVEN, OVEN THERMOMETERS, ETC.
Every recipe you encounter will require a preheated oven. Pay close attention to the temperature called for and invest in an oven thermometer so you'll get accurate temperatures. Cake batter should not sit before baking, because leaveners begin working as soon as they are mixed with liquids and the air in foam batters will begin to dissipate.

WHAT OVEN RACK TO BAKE YOUR CAKE ON:
Place the pan on the oven's center rack. If two or more pans are used, allow at least an inch of space between the pans and two inches between the pans and the walls of the oven for proper heat circulation. DO NOT OPEN THE OVEN during the first half of the baking time. Cold air will interfere with the cake's rising.

Keep a record of baking time for particular recipes in various size pans. You will always want to test each cake to make sure it is ready, but this record will let you know when to begin checking the cake.

Rewrite your recipes in multiples-i.e., 1-1/4 times would list 1 cup as 1-1/4 cup and 2 tablespoons as 2-1/2 tablespoons, etc.

Calculating Ingredients
When planning a wedding cake or other large cake, calculate how much of each ingredient will be needed in the
preparation of multiple recipes. Keep your calculations for future reference when preparing cakes of the same size. SEE: [http://www.baking911.com/howto_recipes_doubletriplecut.htm]

DECORATING TIPS
Preparing Bag
Before beginning to coat or decorate the cake, fill all icing bags with the various colors of icing. Fill a bag with white for borders, etc. Put appropriate tip on each bag and pull other tips that will be used with those same colors.

Consider Similar Colors

CLASSIC RECIPES

When using several colors to decorate one cake or an "assembly line" of several cakes, consider similar icing colors. If pale pink and a deeper rose color will be used, mix the pale pink icing, decorate with that color, then re-mix the same icing with rose coloring to deepen the already-pink color.

Crumb Coat

When decorating several cakes at once, first apply a crumb coat to each cake. Put a small amount of icing in a separate bowl before applying a crumb coat. When you dip back into the bowl, you will not be putting crumbs back into icing that will be used for subsequent coats. Allow crumb coat to crust over (about 15-20 minutes) before applying final coats. Apply two to three coats after the crumb coat for the smoothest possible surface.

Borders

When decorating several cakes at once, use same tip for each cake's borders if possible. If not, apply all borders that use the same tip change tips and complete each cake's borders.

EQUIPMENT TIME SAVERS

Bowls & Paddles

This one item is critical to your business so consider investing in an extra bowl and extra paddle beater. When baking several cakes or a wedding cake, you can save a lot of time by simply changing bowls and paddles when switching from mixing batter to mixing icing or when mixing several batches of batter one after the other.

Washing Up

Cake decorating equipment includes many tiny items that can be tedious to clean. Tiny brushes can be purchased to clean tips and couplers. An easier way to thoroughly clean tips, couplers, and polyester decorating bags is the dishwasher.

Purchase a dishwasher basket at your local baby supplies store where they are marketed for use in washing baby bottle caps and nipples. Drop the basket into the dishwasher and place cake decorating items in the basket. Secure lid tightly and let the dishwasher do the rest.

Cake Rounds

Handling cake layers any larger than 10" can be cumbersome. Layers can tear apart and need to be patched back together or totally remade. When handling cake layers, slide the layer onto a cake round (or rectangle), then move the layer and simply slide it onto the cake.

22

ADDENDUM

When we first wrote this book, the legal aspects were not as complicated as they are today. Local communities are cracking down on home businesses, and friendly competition isn't always so friendly. We've all heard stories about home businesses selling cakes from their kitchen and subsequently being turned in to the local authorities by their brick and mortar competitors. I would have advised her long ago to become legal. Its not as scary as it sounds but it does take work and making some phone calls. Every jurisdiction is different so I don't offer a legal strategy for everyone. What I do encourage though is not to avoid it. Eventually if you want to make enough money to make a living doing this business, you have to be legal.

Legal Considerations for a Home Food Preparation Business

If you are planning your home bakery, catering business or any other home based food preparation business,
you must first do your homework. Each state, county and municipality will have its own regulations, permit and
licensing requirements, and zoning restrictions. To be a responsible business owner, you need to research the laws and guidelines. As a business owner you will also need to think about all the responsibilities that will come along with your business.

I. Legal Expenses/Costs of Your Business
With your new business venture will come the costs of getting the venture off the ground. Besides equipment and ingredient/inventory costs, you will incur costs associated with getting the required license or permit and possible filing fees with the Secretary of State. These fees depend on the business type you choose to set up. Of course these fees will vary from state to state.

A consultation with a business attorney in your local area can vary widely so I would suggest that you call around and ask for referrals from other business owners. You may also wish to call your local bar association because many of them have a referral service. Some attorneys may charge a consultation fee of $50 to $500 but in most cases the fee will be applied to any services that you have them perform. The most common service that an attorney will provide is setting up the business form that you choose and taking care of all the paperwork associated with keeping you legal.

Your attorney can also provide counsel on the liabilities involved in operating your home food prep business and attempt to insulate you from personal liability. In addition, you may want them to prepare some form service contracts tailored to your business so that you have recourse in the event that you don't get paid or a dispute arises over your services. The main thing that an attorney will provide is planning ahead for all of the potential issues that may occur and this is invaluable to a successful business venture.

II. Business Types
When forming a business, you have several business options to choose from. First is a sole proprietorship, which means you are the sole owner. Second is a partnership where you have business partners who share both the profits and liabilities of the business. Third is the corporation. A corporation is a legal entity of which you would then become a shareholder of your business. Through the formation

ADDENDUM

of a corporation you will be insulated from personal liability that may occur in the operation of your business. However, keeping up the formalities of a corporation is a time consuming and expensive proposition. A hot new option among many business formation attorneys these days is the member managed LLC. In a LLC you will enjoy the same protection from personal liability without much of the formalities that are usually associated with a full blown corporation. Depending on what you want out of your business and what services and products you will be offering to your client, you should consult an attorney so that you make an educated choice.

III. Liability Insurance

This is probably the most important area of business ownership that is almost always overlooked at the outset. Most people running an in house business think that their great homeowner's insurance policy will cover them if anything should happen. I implore you to take a look at your policy because this is almost never the case. Insurance companies are very savvy to what people may do in their homes and protect themselves, often times in several different clauses, from the liabilities that are associated with any home food business.

You may also think you do not really need insurance, but think hard about that decision. What happens if you have a fire in your kitchen? What if one of your customers/clients happens to get food poisoning? What about an accident during the transport of your food product? Your homeowner's policy will likely not cover you for this type of damage. Unfortunately, this leaves you and your family's personal assets exposed to the entire liability for injury and damages that you cause. You may also think that you will be able to get your claims past the insurance adjuster without any problem even if it was technically in the operation of your business. Trust me, insurance companies and their investigators know every trick in the book. They will not be easily fooled and you will probably end up the fool without the proper coverage.

Considering the potential liability and the relatively low cost of the coverage it is just inexcusable to not have the proper coverage in place. In some cases you may be able to add a simple endorsement to your homeowner's policy. This can cost you as little as $25.00/month. However, your insurance company may require you to purchase an In- Home Business Policy. Costs of this type of policy vary by business type and insurance company. Finally, you can also get coverage by taking out a Business Owners' Policy which is usually designed specifically for small to medium sized businesses. You will need to make an appointment with your insurance agent to discuss all of your options fully before making a coverage decision.

IV. Zoning Regulations

Remember that as a business owner you will need to check your local municipality or county's zoning regulations. Certain areas within the city limits have restriction that will not allow a business owner to run a business out of the home. Depending on how much traffic your business will be bringing to your home, your business may or may not need to be in commercial zone, a zone specifically set out for business. The punishment for violation of a zoning ordinance may result in a fine, having your business shut down, or even both.

You may be able to go under the radar of city officials for some time, but remember this true story out of West Lafayette, Indiana. The Journal and Courier reported that a home-operated bakery was turned into officials by its neighbors. Even though the neighbors admit that they enjoyed the bakery, all of the increased traffic resulted in real problems. The zoning board in this case deemed the bakery a commercial venture and not able to be operated in a residential area. Consulting an attorney in this regard will save you a big headache in the long run.

V. Tax Considerations

As a responsible business owner, you may be required to collect taxes on your product or service. By consulting an accountant or an attorney, or even looking into your state and local requirements, you can determine whether there is a state sales tax or another type of tax that you must collect in the course of your business.

VI. Business Permits and Licensing
Once you have decided to open your business in your home, you will need to contact your local health department or agency that regulates food and agriculture for your state. The health department or food and agriculture agency will either be responsible for inspection and licensing or will be able to point you in the right direction. However, keep in mind that in some states or areas, a home based food preparation business is not permitted. The following is a list of web addresses for state agencies and other programs available in each state that may be able to help you locate the rules for your state: While on the internet perusing your state's requirements, you may want to look at the following two websites for some further tips on starting your home business:
http://www.powerhomebiz.com; and
http://www.smallbusinessnotes.com/interests/homebusiness.html.

In conclusion, you, the responsible business owner, should take your state's regulations; community's zoning regulations and the liability aspects of owning a business very seriously. If not, you can face serious consequences. As stated earlier, you can face fines, the possibility of being shut down and law suits over injuries or damages which you may be responsible. An attorney can assist you and give you a thorough explanation of what steps you need to take to start your business. A one hour consultation fee may save you thousands of dollars in the future.

23

US GUIDELINES FOR HOMEBASED KITCHENS

Alabama Public Health Dept. Mark Sestak 334-206-5375

Alabama does not allow use of home kitchens. Must be completely separate facility built to state regulations: http://adph.org/environmental/assets/FoodRules2008.pdf
All permitting and inspections handled at county level
Business License: at county level, list: http://www.ador.state.al.us/licenses/authrity.html

Alaska Alaska Department of Environmental Conservation, Division of Environmental Health, Food Safety and Sanitation Program; Kim Stryker (907) 269-7501.

Must have separate commercial kitchen.
Submit plan for approval: http://www.dec.state.ak.us/EH/docs/fss/FoodEstPlanReview.pdf
apply for a permit: http://www.dec.state.ak.us/EH/Application.pdf
fee schedule: http://www.dec.state.ak.us/EH/docs/fss/18%20AAC%2032%20Fees.pdf
State will then inspect and issue permit if everything approved.
Business License: http://www.dced.state.ak.us/occ/buslic.htm

Arizona Must be licensed business entity. Home based businesses must comply with all the same requirements as commercial locations. Per Arizona Department of Health, (602) 542-1023, everything handled at county level.

Arkansas Contact Will Hasting 501-661-2171

Must be separate kitchen that is separate from living quarters and has its own toilet room.
Procedure- submit plans for review and approval. This form gives information on plan requirements and how to establish.
http://www.healthyarkansas.com/rules_regs/guidelines_for_food_establishments_2008.pdf
County health inspector (state employee) will conduct inspection and issue permit of final kitchen.
http://www.arkansas.gov/dfa/income_tax/documents/starting_a-new_business.pdf explains procedures regarding sales taxes etc.
Must also obtain a business license which is handled locally.

California processed food registration (916) 558-1784

Must have separate commercial kitchen. Must contact local health department for licensing and inspection. Business license is handled locally.

Colorado Dan Rifkin State Public Health Dept. 303-692-3644

Must have separate kitchen facility conforming to following regulations:
http://www.cdphe.state.co.us/regulations/consumer/101002RetailFood.pdf
All permitting and inspections handled through county.

START A CAKE BUSINESS TODAY

Must obtain Sales tax license from the state.
Info: http://www.revenue.state.co.us/fyi/pdf/sales24.pdf
Application: http://www.revenue.state.co.us/PDF/cr0100.pdf

Connecticut Dept of Consumer Protection, 860-713-6160
Must be separate facility. Subject to state and local zoning and health laws. State requires plan review and license application. http://www.ct.gov/dcp/lib/dcp/pdf/weights/cpf-96.pdf followed by state inspection. Business license registered with town clerk.

DC Office of Consumer and Regulatory Affairs, 202-442-4576
Chapter 2, section 203 of DC zoning rules, commercial kitchens and home food processing is not allowed in residential properties.   Per DC health Dept, Cannot use home kitchen only commercial kitchens

Delaware Must use completely separate facility. All regulations, instructions and forms contained in this packet: http://www.dhss.delaware.gov/dph/hsp/files/feplanreview0603.txt
Business license:
https://onestop.delaware.gov/osbrlpublic/controller?JSPName=BUSINESSORWITHHOLDINGAGENTYN&op=back

Florida Preparation of food for sale to the public must be in a facility in which there is complete separation of living quarters from food preparation facilities. The food preparation facility must be adequately equipped and fully satisfy all food facility requirements of Chapter 500, F.S., and section 5K-4, F.A.C
The following forms are needed to get a permit:
Make check payable to: FLORIDA DEPARTMENT OF AGRICULTURE AND CONSUMER SERVICES.
Mail check(s) to: FDACS-Food Safety, P.O. Box 6720 Tallahassee, FL 32399-6720.
Must have site plans approved, http://www.doacs.state.fl.us/onestop/forms/14222.pdf
Permit application, http://www.doacs.state.fl.us/onestop/forms/14221.pdf
Business licenses from City or County Occupational License Department.

Georgia Dept. Of Agriculture (404) 656-3621 Mark Norton, mnorton@agr.state.ga.us
Must have separate facility conforming to retail requirements:
http://health.state.ga.us/pdfs/environmental/290-5-14.pdf
Actual applications and permits issued through county but inspections by state.
Business license from city/county.

Hawaii Must have separate facility.
Must submit plan for review:
Oahu:http://hawaii.gov/health/environmental/sanitation/sanitationforms/oahupr.pdf
Hilo:http://hawaii.gov/health/environmental/sanitation/sanitationforms/hilopr.pdf
Kona;http://hawaii.gov/health/environmental/sanitation/sanitationforms/konapr.pdf
Maui:http://hawaii.gov/health/environmental/sanitation/sanitationforms/mauipr.pdf
Molokai:http://hawaii.gov/health/environmental/sanitation/sanitationforms/molokaipr.pdf
Kauai:http://hawaii.gov/health/environmental/sanitation/sanitationforms/kauaipr.pdf

Apply for permit:
Oahu: http://hawaii.gov/health/environmental/sanitation/sanitationforms/oahufe.pdf
Hilo: http://hawaii.gov/health/environmental/sanitation/sanitationforms/hilofe.pdf
Kona: http://hawaii.gov/health/environmental/sanitation/sanitationforms/konafe.pdf
Maui: http://hawaii.gov/health/environmental/sanitation/sanitationforms/mauife.pdf
Molokai: http://hawaii.gov/health/environmental/sanitation/sanitationforms/molokaife.pdf
Kauai: http://hawaii.gov/health/environmental/sanitation/sanitationforms/kauaife.pdf
Business license:
http://hbe.ehawaii.gov/BizEx/home.eb;jsessionid=CE008518CEEF451B8C47A71D90CE0766.liona
create account and then log in. Choose quickfile, Form BB1 General Excise. Fee $22.50

Idaho Environmental Health, 208-327-7499 Must have separate facility.
License application: http://cdhd.idaho.gov/pdfs/food/food_estab_license_app.pdf
Facility requirements: http://cdhd.idaho.gov/pdfs/food/food_estab_requirement.pdf
Plan review and approval form:
http://cdhd.idaho.gov/pdfs/eh/PlanReview%20Form%202005%20Rev%20Mar%202007%20-%202009-07.pdf
Assumed business name must be registered: http://www.idsos.state.id.us/corp/forms/abn.pdf

Illinois Elizabeth Watkins, 217-782-4977
Must have separate commercial facility.
Facility regulations:
http://www.ilga.gov/commission/jcar/admincode/077/07700730sections.html
State considers this a food manufacturer, no licensing requirement at this time. Still subject to inspection. Must report activity to Food Processing Coordinator 217-785-2439.
Business license at county level

Indiana Department of Health, 317-439-9662
Must have separate facility
Plan review form http://www.in.gov/isdh/files/SF50004_R3-6-05.pdf
Application for food service http://www.in.gov/isdh/files/SF49677_R5-05.pdf
Business license: No state filing required for sole proprietorships

Iowa Iowa Department of Inspections and Appeals, Food & Consumer Safety Bureau, Judy Harrison, 515/281-8587. Mary Roaden, Mary.Roaden@dia.iowa.gov
If only baking cakes for sale direct to the consumer no license or inspection required
If selling potentially hazardous (cheesecakes etc) or selling to other retail establishment (restaurant, supermarket) must be licensed and inspected.
Rules regulations and application in attached docs.
No other license required

Kansas Dept. of Agriculture: Steve Moris 785-296-7430, smoris@KDA.STATE.KS.US
Health Inspector: Katherine Robnut 785-207-1288
Per Health department no license or commercial kitchen required. Per DOA as long as sale is non-hazardous product sold to end consumer home kitchen use is acceptable and no license is required.
No separate state business license required.

Kentucky Cabinet for Health and Family Services, Mark Reed (502) 564-7181,
Mark.Reed@ky.gov
Must have separate facility meeting commercial requirements. Attached is there food permit requirements letter.
Business license: must register with the Department of Revenue,
http://revenue.ky.gov/NR/rdonlyres/4A9BEB16-844E-4F8B-B095-8825257E54B5/0/10A100608.pdf
as well as obtain a local business license.

Louisiana Louisiana Dept. of Health, Food and Drug Division. Brian Warren, (225) 342-7517, bwarren2@dhh.la.gov
Must have separate commercial kitchen separated from the residential area by 2 doors.
Guidelines for prospective Manufacturers: http://www.dhh.louisiana.gov/offices/miscdocs/docs-206/food_drug/food_man.pdf
Bakery specific regulations: http://www.dhh.louisiana.gov/offices/miscdocs/docs-206/food_drug/ch5.pdf
Must have plans reviewed: http://www.dhh.louisiana.gov/offices/miscdocs/docs-206/food_drug/plans_review.pdf
Step by step instructions: http://www.dhh.louisiana.gov/offices/publications/pubs-216/How%20To%20Open%20A%20Food%20Establishment%20_RFPHOW_.pdf
Must obtain revenue account number for sales tax:
http://www.rev.state.la.us/forms/taxforms/16019(5_08)F.pdf

Maine_Dept of Agriculture , 207-287-3841, Michelle
May use home kitchen as long as cakes are shelf stable, not cheese cake etc. Must still have Home Processor License.
Application:
http://mainegovimages.informe.org/agriculture/qar/qarforms/food%20and%20fuel%20license%20application.pdf
Complete sections 1,2, and 4.
Business license issued through city/town

Maryland Maryland Department of Health, Food Division 410-767-8400
Bakery and Kitchens regulated at the county level. State only regulates food processing plants.
Business license at county level. Must register trade name with state:
http://www.dat.state.md.us/sdatweb/nameappl.pdf

Massachusetts
Allowed to bake from home kitchen. The following document explains the limitations:
http://www.townofcohasset.org/health/res_kit_brochure.pdf
To sell wholesale or if the operation doesn't conform to the above rules, must be licensed.
Regulations for licensing for home kitchen;
http://www.mass.gov/Eeohhs2/docs/dph/environmental/foodsafety/reskit.pdf
License application: http://www.mass.gov/Eeohhs2/docs/dph/environmental/foodsafety/food_app.pdf
Business license issued by local government

Michigan Dept. of Agriculture. Food and Dairy Administration. Suzanne Kidder Rick,
kidders@michigan.gov, 616-356-0609, mda-info@michigan.gov

Must have separate commercial kitchen and be licensed as a food establishment. License application: http://www.michigan.gov/documents/MDA_FoodEstablishmentLicenseApplicationForm_41243_7.pdf Currently $70 licensing fee.
License and inspection handled at the regional level, following link shows regions and links to get to their offices: http://www.michigan.gov/mda/0,1607,7-125-2961_6860_7306---,00.html
Need a Sales Tax License: Department of Treasury (517) 636-4660 and request a 518 sales tax form.

Minnesota Dept of Agriculture, Food Division, 651-201-6027, Rick.
If only selling to friends and relatives and not advertising can be done out of home kitchen. If operating as a business (selling to others, advertising, selling wholesale) must use separate commercial kitchen and be licensed. Many areas including large municipalities and some counties have regulation delegated to them by the state.
Facility requirements: http://www.mda.state.mn.us/news/publications/food/business&marketing/foodcoderef.pdf
Plan review application: http://www.mda.state.mn.us/news/publications/food/business&marketing/planreviewpacket.pdf
Wholesale Business license: http://www.state.mn.us/license/content.do?mode=license&LicenseID=3930
Retail business license: http://www.state.mn.us/license/content.do?mode=license&LicenseID=4488

Mississippi Dept. of Health
http://www.msdh.state.ms.us/msdhsite/_static/30,3432,77,311.html
Must have separate kitchen.
Regulations: http://www.msdh.state.ms.us/msdhsite/_static/30,0,77,60.html
Procedure flowchart: http://www.msdh.state.ms.us/msdhsite/_static/30,4098,77,311.html
Permit application: http://www.msdh.state.ms.us/msdhsite/_static/resources/432.pdf
No separate state business license required.

Missouri Department of Health.
http://www.dhss.mo.gov/FoodSafety/Faq.html#certified
Must have separate kitchen. All inspections and licensing handled at county/local level.
Missouri food code: http://www.dhss.mo.gov/FoodCode/
Must register 'Fictious business names' with the state.
FAQ about registering: http://www.sos.mo.gov/business/corporations/fictitious_faq.asp
Link for forms doesn't work. Contact information to request them: (573) 751-4153, 1-866-223-6535

Montana Dept. of Public Health, Food and Consumer Safety (406) 444-4735 (Barb)
Requirements of facility: http://www.dphhs.mt.gov/PHSD/Food-consumer/pdf/FDAFoodCode05pdf.pdf
Montana rules: http://www.dphhs.mt.gov/PHSD/Food-consumer/pdf/food_service_establishments_administrative_rule.pdf
Site plan approval requirements http://www.dphhs.mt.gov/PHSD/Food-consumer/pdf/plan_review_requirement.pdf
DPH issues license after inspection.

Nebraska Department of Agriculture, Bureau of Dairies and Foods, (402) 471-2536
If business is less than 3 days per week and no advertising, domestic kitchen is acceptable with no licensing requirement. If more than that must have separate commercial kitchen and obtain a catering license. Licensing handled by regional inspectors and regulations differ.
General guidelines: http://www.agr.ne.gov/pub/daf/preopenlist.htm
If outside Douglas and/or Lancaster County, 402-471-2536

If inside Douglas, (402) 444-7480
If Inside Lancaster County, (402) 441-6280

Nevada Department of Health, 775-684-4200, Nancy Martin
Bureau of Health Protections, Environmental Health Chad Weston 775-687-7539
Must have separate facility.
If not covered by local health department, must have plans reviewed by state,if approved kitchen may be built, they will then inspect and issue a permit.
Food establishment rules: http://www.leg.state.nv.us/NAC/NAC-446.html
Plan review instructions:
http://health.nv.gov/index.php?option=com_content&task=view&id=660&Itemid=1462
Plan review form attached.
Local Business license if sole proprietorship

New Hampshire
It is allowable to bake from a residential kitchen.   Must be inspected and licensed.
Rules: http://www.dhhs.nh.gov/DHHS/FOODSANITATION/ELIGIBILITY/residential-kitchens.htm
License application:
http://www.dhhs.nh.gov/NR/rdonlyres/eoaojwfkpvmixgah5soeue2vly54cgd6eln4rq4fafjo43ekxii5m2drvh
37qcjhg2rpkox6m4ncq4qz5g6h3qczs3h/application.pdf

New Jersey Dept of Health, 609-588-3123.
Must use separate commercial kitchen. If only selling retail direct to consumer licensing is handled at the county level. If selling wholesale to other businesses, must get state license.
Regulations: http://www.state.nj.us/health/eoh/documents/chapter24_effective_1207.pdf
Wholesale license application: http://www.state.nj.us/health/forms/f-29.pdf
Business license: No state license for retail.

New Mexico Must have separate facility. Must submit plans for approval.
Application for plan review:
http://www.nmenv.state.nm.us/fod/Food_Program/documents/PlanReview.pdf
application for food permit:
http://www.nmenv.state.nm.us/fod/Food_Program/documents/ApplicationforFoodPermit.pdf

New York Dept of Agriculture.
Must have separate commercial kitchen. Must be licensed.
License application: http://www.agmkt.state.ny.us/FS/license/pdfs/FSI-303.PDF
Business license issued at county level

North Carolina Use of domestic kitchen is acceptable.
Must call (919) 733-7366 and arrange inspection.
Guidelines: http://www.agr.state.nc.us/fooddrug/food/homebiz.htm
Must register with Dept of Revenue:
http://www.dornc.com/downloads/forms_fillin.php?url=fillin/NCBR_webfill.pdf

North Dakota Dept of Health, Division of Food and Lodging. Kennan, 701-328-1291.

Must have separate commercial kitchen
Regulations:
http://www.ndhealth.gov/FoodLodging/PDF/North%20Dakota%20Food%20Code%202003.pdf
Contact Food Division, 701-328-1291 for Plan review checklist. If plan approved, the will do an inspection followed by a license application.
Business license same.

Ohio Ohio Dept. of Agriculture, Division of Food Safety, 8995 East Main Street, Reynoldsburg, OH 43068. Phone: (614) 728-6250, foodsafety@agri.ohio.gov.
May use home kitchen but must be inspected and licensed. Application given at time of inspection.
Only requirements: no pets in home and no carpet in kitchen.
Fee $10
Business license not required by state for sole proprietorship

Oklahoma Dept of Health. (405) 271-5243
Must have separate commercial kitchen. Licensing and inspections at county level
Rules: http://www.ok.gov/health/documents/Retail%20Foods257-2006.pdf
Business license:
http://busdev3.odoc5.odoc.state.ok.us/pls/portal30/MBLS.RPT_MBLS_LICENSE_4.SHOW?p_arg_names=lid&p_arg_values=180

Oregon

You may use a domestic kitchen subject to the following provisions:
http://www.oregon.gov/ODA/FSD/docs/pdf/pub_domkit.pdf
A plan review is required, http://egov.oregon.gov/ODA/FSD/docs/pdf/pub_pr.pdf. They will then conduct an inspection. If the plan and inspection are approved then an application will be completed at time of license issuance. Business license at county level

Pennsylvania Dept of Agriculture
May use home kitchen for baking.
Guidelines for home kitchen use:
http://www.agriculture.state.pa.us/agriculture/lib/agriculture/foodsafetyfiles/publications/Home_Processing_rev_11-05.doc
You must submit a plan for review if you are selling direct to consumers but not if you are wholesaling.
Applicant letter:
http://www.agriculture.state.pa.us/agriculture/lib/agriculture/foodsafetyfiles/letterforapplicants.pdf
Plan review guidelines:
http://www.agriculture.state.pa.us/agriculture/lib/agriculture/foodsafetyfiles/guidlines.pdf
Plan review application:
http://www.agriculture.state.pa.us/agriculture/lib/agriculture/foodsafetyfiles/applicationforplanreview.pdf
Business license: http://www.paopen4business.state.pa.us/paofb/cwp/view.asp?a=3&q=441248

Rhode Island Dept. of Health, Office of Food Protection. Ernest Julian (401) 222-2749
Can not use home kitchen and they do not license commercial kitchens in residential properties.

South Carolina Dept of Health and Environmental Control, Food Protection 803-896-0640.

Home bakers baking only for family and friends without advertising may use their home kitchen and do not need to have a permit. Otherwise must have separate commercial kitchen.
Regulations: http://www.scdhec.gov/administration/regs/docs/61-25.pdf
Contact local Environmental Health office for permit application, fee $60.
Business license link: https://www3sso.scbos.com//login.aspx?applicationsid=SCBOS

South Dakota Dept of Health, 605-773-3361

Must have separate commercial kitchen.
Food service code: http://legis.state.sd.us/rules/DisplayRule.aspx?Rule=44%3A02%3A07
Application: http://doh.sd.gov/PDF/HPLICENS.pdf
Plan review questionnaire: http://doh.sd.gov/PDF/FOODSRV.PDF
Guidelines: http://doh.sd.gov/HealthProtection/guide.aspx
Step by step instructions: http://doh.sd.gov/HealthProtection/Food.aspx
Business license: contact Department of Revenue and Regulations 605-773-3311

Tennessee Dept of Agriculture, Regulatory Services, Food and Dairy.

May use domestic kitchen for baking if less than 100 units per week.
http://tennessee.gov/sos/rules/0080/0080-04/0080-04-11.pdf
Must have permit: Must request permit from Food and Dairy division. (615) 837-5150 or
Food and Dairy
Regulatory Services Division
Ellington Agricultural Center
Box 40627, Melrose Station
Nashville, TN 37204
Business license issued through municipality or county

Texas Dept of State Health Services, Food and Drug Licensing. Rhonda Henry, (512) 834-6626 x2490.

Must have separate commercial kitchen.
Regulation: http://tlo2.tlc.state.tx.us/statutes/docs/HS/content/pdf/hs.006.00.000434.00.pdf
Many cities and counties have local regulations, if so they are what are followed. If no local regulations then the state licensing is followed.
Contact Food and Drug Licensing Department, 512 834 6626 for correct and up to date information. Due to the number of localities and the frequency of rule changes it will be the only place to get accurate updated information.

Utah Dept of Agriculture and Foods. 801-860-7075. Rebecca Nielson

Allowed to use home kitchen under Cottage Food Rule.
http://ag.utah.gov/regsvcs/CottageFoodCoverLetter.pdf
Law: http://le.utah.gov/~code/TITLE04/htm/04_05011.htm
http://ag.utah.gov/regsvcs/CottageFoodRule080707.pdf
checklist:
guidelines: http://ag.utah.gov/regsvcs/CottageFoodGuidelines.pdf
food processing authorities: http://ag.utah.gov/regsvcs/FoodProcessingAuthorities.pdf
labeling guidelines: http://ag.utah.gov/regsvcs/BasicLabelingGuidelinesForHomeProducedFoods.pdf
One stop licensing and registration for business license: https://secure.utah.gov/osbr-user/user/welcome.html

Vermont Dept of Health.

May use home kitchen that meet bakery rules. Must apply for home bakery license.
Bakery rules: http://healthvermont.gov/enviro/food_lodge/Bakeries.aspx
License application: http://healthvermont.gov/enviro/food_lodge/documents/food_lodge_application.pdf
Business license may also be required from county.

Virginia Department of Agriculture and Consumer Services. 804.786.3520

May use home kitchen. Call and request information packet. Enclosed application is returned and an inspection will be scheduled. Inspection report serves as the permit. Cost $40.
Business license also may be issued by county

Washington Dept. of Agriculture(360) 902-1876, Lucy 360-273-6777

Must have separate facility.
Information regarding facility requirements:
http://agr.wa.gov/FoodAnimal/FoodProcessors/LicenseHandbook.htm#Handbook
Application:
http://agr.wa.gov/FoodAnimal/FoodProcessors/docs/FPLicenseApplicationSept02.pdf
agriculture 'green book', contains some information that may be useful:
http://agr.wa.gov/Marketing/SmallFarm/056-Greenbook-web.pdf

Hardcopies of all handbooks and forms available by calling 360-902-1876 and requesting 'food processors packet'.
Business licensing guide: call (360) 664-1400 or https://fortress.wa.gov/dol/mls/wali/activity.asp

West Virginia

Inspection and permitting of food establishments is the responsibility of the local health department.
http://www.wvdhhr.org/phs/food/index.asp
Business registration packet: http://www.state.wv.us/taxrev/uploads/busapp.pdf

Wisconsin

Must have separate commercial kitchen and be licensed. All license information found here including where to request application packet:
http://www.wisconsin.gov/state/app/license;sesessionid=9SytOsRFCgEHImF3kVG3dS3i?COMMAND=gov.wi.state.cpp.license.command.LoadDetailsCommand&permitId=200012271000000563&permitType=Initial&licenseId=2001010211422154136852
No specific state business license.

Wyoming Dept of Agriculture, Consumer Protection. Linda Stratton 307-777-6592

If only making cakes for 'celebrations' (weddings, parties etc) that are not open to the general public no license is required and the normal residential kitchen is usable.
If making cakes for sale through stores or restaurants must have separate facility.
Facility requirements: http://agriculture.wy.gov/divisions/chs/docs/foodrule2006/2006foodrule.pdf
http://agriculture.wy.gov/divisions/chs/docs/foodservreq.pdf
Business license at county level
Must submit license application, Plan review, and have inspection; all done through local government. Agency dependent on locality.

Made in the USA